Tomorrow I'm Dead

Endorsements

The most amazing story I have ever read. Both sides of the human equation are painted so vividly.

—Elfa Gisla

The horrific events that happened in the Killing Fields brought me to tears. Even more astonishing is how Bun Yom could rise above it all. *Tomorrow I'm Dead* is truly an inspiring story.

—Julie Menkens

I will never complain about anything in my life again … ever!

—Louis Weiss

Bun survived insurmountable odds, encountered dangerous situations repeatedly, yet emerged physically unscathed. That is truly amazing. He had angels protecting him for good reason. In my opinion, he is a hero.

—Barbara Sommers

If Bun's book doesn't instantly change your life, you're already dead.

—Glenn Murphy

Wow! One man overcoming slavery, starvation, grueling labor, loss of family, any one of which could have destroyed him. He not only survived but overcame them all. He lives on a higher plane than most of us ever will.

—Bill Barton

Tomorrow I'm Dead

A MEMOIR

Bun Yom

TOMORROW I'M DEAD
A MEMOIR

iUniverse books may be ordered through booksellers or by contacting:

iUniverse
1663 Liberty Drive
Bloomington, IN 47403
www.iuniverse.com
1-800-Authors (1-800-288-4677)

Because of the dynamic nature of the Internet, any web addresses or links contained in this book may have changed since publication and may no longer be valid. The views expressed in this work are solely those of the author and do not necessarily reflect the views of the publisher, and the publisher hereby disclaims any responsibility for them.

Any people depicted in stock imagery provided by Thinkstock are models, and such images are being used for illustrative purposes only. Certain stock imagery © Thinkstock.

Back cover photo by Dean Duby.
Map by Ryan Chandler.
All photos courtesy of Bun Yom or the Cambodian Freedom Army.

ISBN: 978-1-4917-5850-2 (sc)
ISBN: 978-1-4917-5851-9 (e)

Library of Congress Control Number: 2015902249

Print information available on the last page.

iUniverse rev. date: 4/27/2015

To every human being—be peaceful and kind to one another, always, no matter the circumstance.

—Bun Yom

A Map of Bun's World

Foreword

During the early 1960s, a Cambodian named Pol Pot became the leader of an underground Communist party that opposed Cambodia's new royal monarchist government. As his party grew, Pol Pot formed a resistance army in the jungles of Cambodia, known as the Khmer Rouge (Red Cambodians).

In 1970, US military forces entered Cambodia in an attempt to expel North Vietnamese rebels who had fled into Cambodia. Over the next five years, the North Vietnamese were successfully driven out of major Cambodian cities, along with several hundred thousand Cambodian peasants, most of whom fled to the city of Phnom Penh for refuge. Many of these North Vietnamese escaped to the surrounding jungles and allied themselves with Pol Pot's Khmer Rouge. As the Khmer Rouge strengthened, their plan to overtake Phnom Penh intensified.

Having witnessed their friends and families die during the Vietnam War, struggling Cambodian peasants, desperate for hope, began to believe in the social utopia promised by Pol Pot, promises he said would bring them peace and a better life. Pol Pot's army, which was now well supplied by Communist China, grew exponentially and soon gained the allegiance of many of these displaced Cambodians.

By 1975, US troops had withdrawn from Cambodia, leaving the people defenseless against Pol Pot's army, the Khmer Rouge. The Khmer Rouge soon controlled Phnom Penh and much of southern Cambodia. With no military force to oppose them, the Khmer Rouge initiated one of the most atrocious genocide campaigns the world has ever known.

At this time, many of the well-educated, wealthy Cambodians were residing in modern cities near the Thailand border. It was in these cities and surrounding fields and jungles that the Khmer Rouge, fueled by fierce contempt for the wealthy and educated, unleashed their greatest brutality. These were the worst of the Killing Fields. It was here that fourteen-year-old Bun (pronounced "Boon") Yom was taken from his parents and forced to work as a slave in conditions so inhumane it seemed only death could free him.

The Khmer Rouge's brutality would soon rival Nazi Germany's attempt to eradicate the Jews from Europe as the single most horrifying act of violence ever committed against a nation's people. Over the next four years, two million people (one-fifth of the Cambodian population) were enslaved and either murdered, starved, or worked to death.

After three years in the Killing Fields, seventeen-year-old Bun Yom escaped from the Khmer Rouge and became a Freedom Fighter. Using his wisdom, selfless courage, and unprecedented compassion, Bun rescued thousands of Cambodian people and soon became the Cambodian Freedom Army's greatest soldier.

Those who do not remember the past are condemned to repeat it.
—George Santayana

Keith Mark Johnson
Ellensburg, WA
July 2004

Preface

When I was thirteen years old, I had my freedom and my family. A year later, the Khmer Rouge took over and changed my life forever. I was taken from my parents and forced to work as a slave in the Killing Fields. Most of the young people of western Cambodia died in those fields. This book is for anyone who might benefit from learning about the hard lives so many Cambodian people endured. I hope that by reading my story of survival they can learn to appreciate their own lives.

I wrote for all the young people who would benefit from learning about the atrocities we experienced in the Killing Fields and how, even then, we still helped people.

I want young people to know that when I became a Freedom Soldier, it didn't matter whether there was fighting or not, food or not, sleep or not, rain or not. I always tried to help the people and get them new lives, lives away from the starvation and suffering.

I want young people everywhere to understand that war is a terrible thing. I fought in a war for five years—with bombs, mines, and bullets every day, never knowing when I would die. I slept in jungles and fields with dead bodies. I saw too many people suffer because of young soldiers with guns and bombs. War is a terrible thing.

My advice to all young people: Stay in school. Listen to good people who can give you guidance. Learn to be strong and to trust yourself. Always do the right thing for yourself and for others.

Today, this world is a small place. All corners of the earth have humans who are trying to survive. It is important that kids learn about these people too.

Some people do not appreciate what they have. I hope these readers can learn some good things from my story.

To all people everywhere, try to help out in any way you can. That is why you are here.

I arrived in the United States with not one penny, not a word of English, and only the clothes I was wearing. By working hard, I now have my own home, a family, my own business, and many good friends.

It took twenty years before I was ready to write about my years in the Killing Fields. Now, for the sake of all young people everywhere, it is time to share my story.

Hang in there. Do the right thing, and don't ever give up.

Thank you for your support.

PART ONE

Kill Us Slowly

1 My Parents' Story

My father was born in Thailand on April 10, 1926. He came to Cambodia in 1944. That was the year France and Thailand were fighting each other in World War II. The French were fighting in Cambodia as well as Vietnam and Laos. Thailand fought the French army until they left Cambodia, and then Thailand took part of Cambodia's land and its people.

My father, Yom, and his brother, Noun, went to Cambodia on foot, fifty miles through the jungle and two days' traveling time. My father was eighteen at the time. The two brothers searched for a way to make money and returned to Thailand by foot many times. This became a way of life for the next ten years.

The jungles of this humid tropical region were tough to travel through. The trails were narrow and went up and down through forests of rubber, banana, palm, coconut, kapok, and banyan trees.

The wildlife was like a zoo, with elephants, tigers, monkeys, parrots, cranes, and poisonous snakes. In the rainy season, every leaf was covered with leeches—toothpick-sized worms that latch onto animals and people to suck their blood. The leeches swelled up to the size of a thumb shortly after attaching to a warm spot on the skin.

When my father was twenty-seven, he met a beautiful woman, my mother, Heng, in Cambodia. She too searched for ways to make a living. They got married in Cambodia in 1954. My uncle He Ty (pronounced "Hie Tee") took care of the marriage and the wedding. After the wedding, they returned to Thailand so my mom could meet my father's family and they could remarry, because a Thai wedding was not considered official in Cambodia at that time.

Both my parents worked very hard. Food was short with two people to support. They both dug for rubies—red, white, blue, and brown rubies. This was very hard work. A person-sized hole had to be dug straight down into the ground, just big enough to crawl down into, with one's elbows touching each side. If one was lucky, the holes had to be dug only five feet deep before one found rubies.

But many holes went ten and sometimes thirty feet down into the earth. For these, small holes were cut into the sides of the earth, like steps. The digging was done with a crowbar, and the loosened stones and dirt were then hauled up with a bucket on a rope. When the actual vein of rock was as much as thirty feet below the surface, pulley systems were rigged to haul out the dirt by hand. This took at least two people for each hole.

Once the dirt was removed, the soil was put in a shaker. My parents would shake and shake and shake, hoping to find a ruby. Many people did this very hard form of work for a living.

Some days, they found a stone that was big enough to sell and provide food for two months; some days, nothing. These rubies were sold in Thailand. Those days, my parents went back and forth through the jungle on foot many times.

In 1955, my mom had her first child. His name was Phon (pronounced "Pon"). My mother stayed home with the baby while my father returned to work. When my brother was one and a half years old, my mother took him to Thailand to visit Grandmother and Grandfather. My mother then returned to help my father work, carrying my brother on her side. When he cried, she moved him onto her back in a cloth sling, where he could either see his surroundings or sleep.

The house they lived in at the time was a very poor house, with holes in the walls and a leaky roof made of bamboo poles and large leaves. The sides of the house had leaves and bamboo bars. When it rained, water streamed in, and they tried to keep the baby dry. There was no bathroom. No running water. No electricity. No dishes. No furniture. Nothing. Poor people had to work hard just to stay alive. There was no welfare system in Cambodia. They lived at a subsistence level. There was no margin for error. The choice was to work very hard or risk starvation.

I was born in Pailin, Cambodia, on June 20, 1960, the second son, named Bun Yom. I was born in my parents' humble house. That day, there was a bad windstorm that took the roof away. Everything was soaking wet, including me.

My mother returned to work, digging for rubies, two weeks after I was born. My five-year-old brother took care of me as my parents worked nearby. In Cambodia, the practice of young children taking care of babies still goes on today. When I was about nine years old, my mother said to me, "When you grow up, you will bring a lot of luck to me, because we found a large red ruby the first day I returned to work after you were born." The ruby was perhaps five karats. This precious stone was worth 5,000 baht (pronounced "bot," Thai currency). At that time, one could buy a house, open a business, and still have some money left over for 5,000 baht.

They took the ruby to Thailand, sold it, returned to Cambodia, and bought a house with land. With the money she had left, Mother bought rubies from other people. These were taken to Thailand and sold. She was now a businesswoman, with no formal education or schooling, with neither a teacher nor the ability to read or write. She figured out how to run a business all by herself.

My father took my mother to the places she needed to go on their motorcycle. One day, my dad was taking Mom back from her work. As they approached a wooden bridge at a high speed, my mom screamed, "Stop! Stop!" and my father screamed back, "I have no brakes!"

Father turned the motorcycle away from the bridge, and they plunged into a water ditch. My mom hit her head on a rock in the water, and my father was bruised from head to toe. People from the village saw this and raced over to help pull the motorcycle out. With the motorcycle now full of mud and broken down, they traveled by bicycle the next day, with my mom sitting on the seat as my dad pedaled. This was a bit safer form of travel, since the bike had a workable hand brake.

In 1961, another baby was born at the new house—a girl named Bo Pha (pronounced "Bo Paw"). Again there was no hospital. A family doctor came to the house to deliver the baby. The cost was 100 raels (Cambodian currency). Our family was now a mother, a father, two sons, and a daughter.

My mother opened a small grocery store and restaurant at the front of the house. My older brother was old enough to take care of the kids and business at home, which was good help. By six o'clock each morning, Mom would be in the store/restaurant, stocking the shelves, caring for the grocery customers, handling the cash transactions, and cooking for people who came to eat. My father would sweep the floor, wait on the tables, and bus the dirty dishes. People returning from digging rubies would drop by in the afternoon to sell to my parents whatever they had found. It was a place where they could turn their day's work into cash. Soon, many people knew where to stop to sell their day's work, which they sometimes then spent for groceries at the family store. This process helped to restock shelves as my parents' business grew. For four years, this business continued to grow and prosper.

In 1965 another brother, Cole He (pronounced "Kola Hee"), was born. There were now four children. The store was still going strong. When Cole He was one year old, he became ill with hives for three months. Mother stayed home to take care of him, boiling roots and bathing him with cool water to bring relief. Father returned to digging rubies with my oldest brother.

In 1970, my parents sold the house, and we moved to Jra, Cambodia. Four Buddhist monks held a blessing at the new house. They uttered prayers designed to bring luck into the house. During the prayers, they sprinkled water in every part of the house. After this, we moved into the house and ate together. Once again, one week later, my mother opened a combination grocery store and restaurant in our house. She cooked and sold groceries until noon every day. In the afternoon, she bought rubies from the diggers.

My sister was now nine years old and sold banana wraps on the street to people on their way to work. Mom prepared these wraps, which were banana leaves filled with rice, coconut milk, and sugar, at six o'clock each morning. Noodle soup and rice soup were served for breakfast.

On the weekends, my parents would go to Thailand by car, a four-hour drive, to sell rubies, while my siblings and I stayed at home and worked in the store. When our parents returned, the store was restocked, using money from the ruby sales in Thailand.

In 1971 my parents closed the store and took a two-month vacation with our family to Thailand to see the grandparents, cousins, and relatives. We stayed at Grandmother's house in Chanthaburi, Thailand. After we returned to Cambodia, my uncle, He Ty, took me and my brother Cole He to his farm outside Pailin, a few miles from Jra, where he raised fruit for a living. My mother, father, sister, and brother Cole were left at home.

My mom had another baby in 1975, a boy named Chhay Thay (pronounced "Chie Tow"). Six months after Chhay was born, the Khmer Rouge came and took over Cambodia, telling everyone in the cities to get out of their homes.

On that day in April 1975, my mom, dad, brothers, sister, and I were ordered out of our house, told to pack nothing, and forced at gunpoint to march away toward the jungle. We were together there for two days and two nights. We had no food or supplies. After two days, a Khmer Rouge soldier came and said, "Come out and get some food." My mom said to me, Phon, and Bo Pha, "You go with the soldier to get food." We went with them. The next day, a Khmer Rouge soldier separated my brother and me from my sister, and then, me from my brother. I did not see them or my parents for nine years.

This was the day our lives changed forever.

2 *My School Years*

In 1966, my parents took me to my first day of school, and we had a picture taken. My parents told my teacher three things that day. They said, "This is our kid. Make sure he stays in school. Don't break his bones, cut his skin, or poke out his eyes."

On my first day of school, I was in twelfth grade, because grades in Cambodia are numbered from twelfth to first, instead of first to twelfth. School was from 8:00 a.m. to 5:00 p.m. We wore school uniforms—the boys wore blue short pants and white shirts; the girls wore white blouses and blue skirts. In class, we sat one boy and one girl to each table. The teacher told us to make sure our clothes were clean and neatly tucked in. There was a blackboard, books, and a globe in the classroom, and the same teacher taught us all day. There was no toilet at the school. Kids just went off into the nearby jungle to pee or poop.

In 1969, my parents took the whole family to Thailand to visit relatives for about two weeks. The time I spent in Thailand with my parents was very special for our family. We got to see our grandmother and two uncles after being apart for three years.

When we returned to Cambodia, I went back to school. I was placed in ninth grade. I only needed to go to school for three months. The teacher told me that they wanted to send me to seventh grade. This skipping of two grades was exceptional. That day, when I got home and told my parents that I was promoted to a higher class, they took me to the teacher to find out why I was not going through each step, year by year. The teacher said that I was a very smart kid and that I shouldn't have to take the classes I already knew. After my parents heard that, they thanked the teacher for letting me pass all those grade levels. Then my parents went back home.

My teacher gave me some rewards at the end of the year, including a pencil, notebook, pen, and eraser. I said, "Thank you for all these gifts." When I got home, my parents asked me, "Where did you get all these supplies?" I replied, "I got them from my teacher as rewards." My parents didn't believe me. They said, "You must not be telling the truth. Did you steal them from somebody?" The next morning, my parents took me to the teacher, who said, "It is true. These were special gifts for Bun. If any child does really well in school, he gets rewarded."

After that, my teacher gave me even more homework. I had seven classes each day: reading, math, writing, old Cambodian, art, sports, and history. Each day, we students were given the option of which sport we would practice. Some kids liked to run. Some liked to play ball sports. I chose to learn tae kwon do. This sport involves a combination of karate, kick boxing, and judo. We learned tricks on how to defend ourselves. By the end of the year, our teacher had taught us how to fight. This was fun. At first, I fought one-on-one with another student. If I knocked my opponent down, the teacher sent out two more. I made it until I was up against four, but that was too much. They beat me down to the ground. There were no pads on the ground or on my body. When I got kicked or hit, it hurt. At the end of the school year, there was a test against other classes to see who had learned tae kwon do the best. I got a good grade on this test. The teacher told me I did very well and then sent me out to fight a bigger guy. That year, I earned a white belt.

Some days when I went to school, my teacher would write Cambodian letters on the board, and we students would copy them. When we were finished copying, we would take it home to practice, almost like homeschooling. I would wake up at three in the morning to study what I had learned in school the day before. I would have to remember all the work that we did, because the teacher wanted us to learn how to remember the homework that he gave us. Then, when we went back to school, our teacher would call us up one by one to tell the class what we had learned yesterday. This is how the teacher made sure the students studied. If we missed one word, we would get hit with a stick.

One day when I missed a lot of words, my teacher hit me with a stick and blood came up from the welt. The teacher asked, "Did you copy your homework from someone else?"

I answered, "Yes, I did."

"Why didn't you study the assignment?"

I replied, "I had no time. I had to work at my Uncle Hy Te's farm. He needed my help to do irrigation."

At the end of the school day, my teacher took me to my parents and told them that he had hit me because I missed a lot of words. My parents didn't say too much; they just took me into the living room and hit me some more.

After that night, I thought about why I had made those mistakes. I remembered that my teacher said to study at night and never miss a word. From that day on, I never missed another word in school.

Once, when I got to school a half hour late, my teacher told me to go outside and run around the school five times. After I finished running, my teacher told me to never be late again, and I never was.

The next year, in 1969, I went to school thinking I was a little tougher because I was in fifth grade now. I was only nine years old and already in the equivalent of eighth grade in the United States. In eighth grade (fifth grade Cambodian), I had to go to school for three months. There was more homework, and it was harder. I would still do the usual work, as I had the year before, but I would wake up to study my homework at one in the morning, and when I went to school, I made sure I was never late. Then, when I got to school, I would take tests and finish projects.

My teacher took me to my parents one day after school. I was scared to death because I thought that I might get hit again. The teacher said nothing along the way, giving me no hint of what was the matter, and I had no idea what I had done wrong. I thought, *What could it be? What did I do wrong?* When we got to my parents' house, my teacher knocked on the door and asked if he could come in. My parents were alarmed. "Is Bun in trouble?" they asked.

My teacher told them, "No, this time Bun did not get in trouble. I actually have good news. Bun did very good at school. He did not miss school, he got all his homework done, and he scored highly on tests that were very challenging. I think that maybe Bun is too smart for his class and needs to go up two more classes." That would be the third grade, equivalent to tenth grade in the United States.

Of course school got much harder; plus, I had to work for my uncle after school each day. At the end of the school year, my teacher gave me awards (pencils and other school supplies) because I had done so well, which I used in school. In the tae kwon do tests, I was able to defeat four opponents. My legs were black-and-blue and bumpy after the test, but I was very proud and earned a black belt. Later that day, my teacher went to my house to tell my parents how well I had done and the awards I had received. My parents happily replied, "Thank you. This is good news, but Bun needs to go to school some more." This particular school was not funded by the government. Parents had to pay tuition for their children to attend.

In 1970, my uncle took me and my brother Cole to the farm where he lived. Together, we watered the fruit trees. My brother then stayed at the farm while I went to school. When I came back from a day of classes, I would help him.

In 1971, my classes were even harder. Everything was extremely difficult: my homework, tests, and what to remember. My teacher would keep an eye on those who were smart and those who were not. Those who didn't get a lot of answers right would get spanked.

In 1972, I only went to school for three months. The teacher gave a test to only the better students, and on that day, my name was on the list. The next morning after the test, three people were to take an even harder test, and once again my name was on the list.

At the end of 1972, my teacher told my parents that I needed to go to a higher school. He said I was doing exceptional work in math and languages. This higher school was very difficult, however, so I worked very hard in school and studied even harder at night.

In 1973, school again became more challenging. Close to the end of that year, my schooling was almost over. This was the year I remembered watching my desk shake as B-52 planes flew overhead on their way to North Vietnam. When I would go out on the playground, I could see the white underbellies of the massive bombers. My teacher told us not to worry. He told us there was always war in Vietnam.

I was worried all the time that year—I was afraid that North Vietnam would invade Cambodia—but I hung in there. We had to take very difficult exams, but I made the list each time. I would try my best on the tests and then make the next list, only to take harder and harder tests. This was schooling, Cambodian-style.

In 1974, I was fourteen years old. My favorite sports were soccer and practicing tae kwon do. Some kids were really good at tae kwon do and could go eight against one. The most I could defend still was four. These tests left my body bruised. When my dad asked me how I got the bruises and I replied, "I got kicked playing my sport," he smiled and said, "That's good." He knew that in Cambodia, people had to know how to fight. There were no police to protect you. Knowing how to defend yourself was very important. Sometimes the fights were with fists and feet, sometimes with knives. I knew how to take care of myself in all kinds of fighting.

We were taught to fight with sticks. I liked to fight with the long sticks, as I would hit my head too many times with the short ones. We also learned how to break bricks and "fly" through the air (jumping while kicking).

When I got home from school and my parents saw my bruises, they boiled tree roots in water and soaked my legs. I would soak my legs in a tub for one hour, and the swelling would go down. My father was very good at taking care of our injuries. He helped us with broken bones, bruises, and other things. He knew the jungle medicine and other tricks that he had learned in Thailand.

Those were happy years. What was about to happen to me, my family, and my country, however, no human on earth could have foreseen. The US soldiers were leaving Cambodia, and the Khmer Rouge army was moving in to steal everything.

3   *Angry Kids with Guns*

One day in April 1975, I woke up and heard guns everywhere. This day, I was at my uncle's farm. It did not take long for my uncle to come back to the farm. He said, "Something is wrong. I am going to get in my car and go to Thailand with my family and your brother Cole He."

"May I go with you?" I asked.

He replied, "I have no room, but I will come back for you. Don't worry. I will return to pick up another load of family."

I waited and waited all day, but he did not come back. I sat by myself, listening to the guns. I was frightened and confused.

Later that day I saw my parents walking the few miles toward the farm. I told them that they had to stay on the farm because my uncle would come back here to find us. My parents and siblings stayed at the farm for one night. We still could hear the guns far away. My parents wondered if the Vietnam War was now in Cambodia. They did not know about the Khmer Rouge. When they'd left their home in Jra, they hadn't taken anything but the clothes and jewelry they'd been wearing. The Khmer Rouge soldiers had given them no time. We waited in fear that night, hoping my uncle would come back for us with his tiny Toyota. While we waited, we lost our one chance to escape the Khmer Rouge. My uncle got his family and my brother Cole He safely to Thailand, but he was not allowed to return for the rest of us. When he drove the Toyota back to the border, it was closed.

He had no idea what was going on. None of us did. We had no way of knowing how costly that single night's delay would be.

The night was quiet, and we all were able to sleep. We were awoken by the sound of gunfire, and it kept increasing all morning. From all corners of the farm, I could hear shots, both loud and soft.

My dad looked outside of the house to see what was happening. When he came back inside, he said, "There are a lot of people walking on the roads—thousands of people walking. I asked a man what was happening, and he said to get out of our home because a war was going to begin with Vietnam."

Soon, the Khmer Rouge approached the house in vehicles, yelling over megaphones for everyone to get out of their houses. My father said to us, "Get out now, before the Vietnamese bombs hit us." We all got out and started walking on the streets with everyone else.

As I walked, I saw thirteen- and fourteen-year-old children wearing green uniforms. I asked someone, "Who are those kids wearing green uniforms?"

"They are Communists called the Khmer Rouge," the man answered.

I did not understand what he meant because we had never had Communists in Cambodia. As we continued to walk, these kid soldiers pointed guns and yelled at people to get out of their houses and walk faster. They said, "All people, do not worry about your houses. Just walk out with one pair of clothes. You will be gone just for a few days, and then you will come back to your houses."

And so we walked. These soldiers were about the same age and size as I was. I was afraid they might shoot at any minute. I didn't know what might set them off.

Later that morning, I saw a family plead with these Khmer Rouge that they had forgotten things in their home and that they needed to go back and get them. The Khmer Rouge said to not go back. When the people turned around to head for their home, the Khmer Rouge shot them all with pistols and AK-47s. They left the bodies where they had fallen. This terrified the rest of us who were walking on the street. We did not know what was going on. There was nothing we could do for the slain family, but we knew if we turned around and didn't walk straight they might shoot us too.

Everywhere was the sound of gunfire. The Khmer Rouge were shooting people, as well as shooting over our heads and ordering people to keep walking away from their homes. We were all scared to death.

That day, I saw thousands and thousands of people walking out of Pailin. Everyone walked all day and through the night. They hoped that they would get to go back home.

About one in the morning, the moon rose. My brother Chhay, who was six months old, would not stop crying because he had not been fed any milk. My parents tried to find some type of rice or food for our family because we all were so hungry from walking for twenty-four hours straight. My sister, brother, and I also tried to find some food for Chhay so he would stop crying. All we could do was ask other people for food, but they did not have enough even for themselves.

A group of Khmer Rouge soldiers walked toward my family because they had heard Chhay cry. They said, "Don't let your baby cry, because if the Vietnamese hear that, they will kill everybody. When we come back, if we hear the baby crying, we will take the whole family out on the street and kill them."

After that, my siblings, Bo Pha and Phon, and I watched for the Khmer Rouge. If the soldiers came close, my sister would tell me, and I would stuff cloth into Chhay's mouth. As soon the Khmer passed us, I would take the cloth out of his mouth. Chhay cried all day—he would not stop crying. His belly was swollen from hunger. We kids split up to ask people on the road for food, but we had no luck finding any.

Then the Khmer Rouge announced over a megaphone, "Do not back up or stop unless we tell you to stop."

Two hours later, we saw many dead people on the side of the road—adults, boys, girls, and soldiers. It looked like they had been killed that day. Whole families were piled one upon another, lying where they had fallen. We were shocked by the sight of dead people heaped on the side of the roads like that. None of us understood why they had been killed or why we were being forced away from our homes.

We walked all day through the hot, steaming jungle. When I looked around, I saw thousands of people walking behind us and thousands in front of us. Later, I saw the Khmer Rouge had brought in more troops. This second shift of young soldiers were not nice to anyone. Some of these kids were so small that their AK-47s almost touched the ground when slung over their shoulders. When they shot the guns into the air, they were almost knocked down.

I looked at these angry kids, knowing that I could beat up any of them, but there was nothing I could do. They were yelling at old people, pointing their guns, and screaming at us to keep moving. "Old lady, get your butt up!" they screamed.

This made me mad, but I knew that if I said anything, they would shoot me. I marched on with my head down, the jungle heat sticking to my skin, and my heart trembling with fear.

I kept thinking, *Where are we going? Why are they yelling at us? Why are these kids carrying guns and shooting people?*

The young and the old—men, women, and children—were forced to march away from their homes. I trekked along with them, not knowing what was to come.

4 The Lines

Late that evening in April 1975, a Khmer Rouge soldier with a megaphone shouted, "Everyone take a rest. Tomorrow morning, we will start walking again. You will all be separated, because if you all stay in a group together, it is not good. If the Vietnamese army sees our group walking, they will kill us all."

This was a lie. The Vietnamese had not yet invaded Cambodia.

The next day, the Khmer Rouge said they needed all the kids to go get food. They announced over their megaphones, "If anybody has a boy or girl, we need them, because we need kids to go with us." My mother and father said they would send me, my brother, and my sister. My youngest brother, only six months old, would stay with my parents. Then my brother, sister, and I walked away from our mom and dad. We hoped we would be able to bring food to our parents. All the parents hoped that their children would bring food to them too. The Khmer Rouge marched us off into the jungle.

After we were away from our parents for three days, the Khmer Rouge called all the kids together—there were probably two or three hundred around me. Across the fields were other groups of kids. I could look up and see all black heads in the jungle. We were all very hungry; we had not been given any food during those three days of nonstop walking.

The Khmer Rouge jumped down from a big truck and called out

"boy" and then "girl" as they separated the girls from the boys. My sister went one way, and my brother and I went the other way. I called to my sister, "If you get food, go to Mother and Brother first. And if I get food, I will go to them first." That was the last time I saw my sister until 1997, in Tacoma, Washington.

Then Phon and I walked away together. I saw hundreds of big dump trucks lined up along a jungle road. I thought that maybe the trucks were there to haul the food back to our parents. The Khmer Rouge said, "All you guys—don't go anywhere."

My brother and I stayed tightly together all that day. That day just happened to be my fifteenth birthday.

They called the boys one by one and asked each of us questions. They asked, "Whose son are you? Are you a student? Are you rich? Are you Chinese?"

I listened to them ask questions to some of the kids, and I heard one say, "My parents have a grocery store."

When the Khmer Rouge asked, "Are you a student?" and he said yes, they sent the kid to a truck.

Then they asked another one, who replied that he was a farmer. He was sent to another truck. After they were all questioned, they were taken away in five trucks. Still more trucks were in the line.

As I stood there waiting for my turn, a thirteen-year-old boy came up and said to me, "I have just escaped from the 'educated' dump truck. The Khmer Rouge drove off with the truckload of people and headed straight for a giant-sized hole that was carved out with a bomb. The people in the truck were then dumped straight into the hole, which was full of dead bodies. When I saw the hole, I jumped out of the truck and escaped into the jungle. I made my way back to tell you not to say you have education or money." Now, he stood in line with us. He was a very brave young man.

They called my brother, and he said he was a farmer. He was sent to a truck. Then they asked me, and I said, "I am a farmer. I help my uncle. I am from Pailin." They sent me to the same truck as Phon.

We talked quietly on the truck. I said, "They asked us to get food for our parents. Three days have passed. Where is the food?" Phon said he did not know. I looked back as the trucks took off. A lot of kids were still lined up. The Khmer Rouge said we would take a break at six in the evening.

That evening, we climbed out of the trucks and were told to wait. The Khmer Rouge took the trucks away. Thousands of us waited there. I looked around to see where my brother had gone, but I could not see him—there were too many people in the jungle. It was hot and humid, and I did not know what was to come.

That night, I thought about my mom, my dad, and my baby brother and how they thought we were bringing them food. I didn't know how they were doing. I wondered what they might be thinking. I remembered my family walking away from my uncle's house together.

The next morning, the Khmer Rouge came up to me, pointed an AK-47 toward the south, and said, "You go that way." I began to walk with a large group of people.

The Khmer Rouge said to keep walking and not stop. Two hours later, I saw another Cambodian group stopped in front of our group. These kids were taking some kind of test, one at a time. After each person took the test, he or she was told to sit in different sections. We saw a lot of Khmer Rouge with guns, walking around the people.

Then the Khmers started calling us up, one by one again. That day, I figured out that something was terribly wrong. We still hadn't picked up food for our parents, and now, after three days of walking, we were taking tests.

The Khmer Rouge made us walk into a tent. The test they gave was simple; they asked if you were a lawyer, teacher, doctor, student, or Chinese or white. If you said yes to any of those, you were sent one way; farmers were sent another way.

Eventually, the Khmer Rouge sat me down and asked me questions, face-to-face. Nighttime was approaching. The boy interrogating me was only twelve or thirteen. He looked angry and had an AK-47 slung over his shoulder. He asked me where I was born.

I said, "Pailin."

Another soldier shouted at me, "What do your parents do?"

I told them that my mother and father were farmers. They asked me where my farm was. My mind raced with fear. I told them the farm was five miles from Pailin and that I worked for my uncle. I was making it up.

They asked me, "Do you go to school?"

"No."

"Do you have any schooling?"

"No," I lied again.

They asked me why I hadn't gone to school. I said it was because we had a farm, we were poor, and I had a lot of brothers and sisters I had to take care of while my parents went to work. They got in my face, red-eyed and angry, and asked me if I was lying.

I said, "No, I'm telling the truth."

Another face came forward and screamed more questions. "Are you Chinese? Are your parents Chinese?"

I was shaking. I said, "No, they are Cambodian—born in Cambodia."

Finally, the soldiers said, "Okay. This time we'll let you go."

I said, "Thank you," and walked away, looking at the ground to make sure they didn't call me again. I wondered what was going to happen to all these people. We had been given enough food to last four days, but then what?

After that, they sent me to a spot where there were uneducated people. Then they went to a group of teachers with students and told this group to sit somewhere else but not with my group.

I heard the Khmer Rouge say to these people that if their parents had opened a grocery store, they were to go to a different spot. I did not understand why the Khmer Rouge were doing this. I wondered why they were taking educated people one way and uneducated people another way.

I took a look around and saw thousands and thousands of people sitting in the field, waiting for the next set of orders from these angry children soldiers.

5 *Kill Us Slowly*

Late that day, the Khmer Rouge finished their testing. We were told to line up again. I saw dump trucks and supplies waiting in the field. They called our group over and said, "Take off your clothes, rings, watches, necklaces, and earrings."

People with glasses were able to keep them so they could see. I wondered why the Khmers took all the colored clothes off the people. I wondered why there were thousands of people lined up to take off their jewelry. They put all the jewelry into big rice bags.

The Khmer Rouge lined up in front of us. Each person in line was given one pair of white pants and a white shirt. After that, we were given our work equipment. This consisted of a single-blade shovel and two buckets attached to a bamboo bar to sling over our shoulders. We were all dressed in white, and the young Khmer Rouge soldiers were dressed in green.

They all carried guns. The Khmer Rouge said to us, "Everybody, do not worry. We have taken all the colored clothes away from the rich people. We don't need all that stuff from rich people."

They said that from now on, all people were the same. There were no more rich people. We would all eat the same and dress the same. The Khmer Rouge said, "We are together right now. We don't need rich people, we don't need doctors, and we don't need smart people. We will take care of you."

The Khmer Rouge then told us we would stay here until the next day. They set up thirty people in one group. There was no leader. Everyone was the same.

After they set up thousands and thousands of people in groups, they told my crew that tomorrow we would go to work. They reminded us to take care of all equipment, or we would be in trouble.

We were marched to a truck and then taken to a different place, about an hour's drive away. That night, when I went to sleep, I had to lie on branches on the ground. I had never done that before. I had always had a house and a bed to sleep on. This was the rainy season. The ground was muddy. I was wet day and night.

I thought of my mother. She did not know where I was or if I was still alive. If I was killed, she would never know.

Early the next morning, the Khmer Rouge called everyone to wake up. They said, "We have to go forward. All of you people line up, and then we will take off."

We then walked for four hours straight. I was starving. Everyone else was hungry too, but the Khmer Rouge kept making us walk. They said, "Let's walk one more hour and then we will take a break."

An hour later, we came to a clearing in the jungle that had a lot of Khmer Rouge soldiers standing there. We were told to stop right there, and we would be given something to eat.

Then one Khmer Rouge group came out with plates and bowls in their hands. Behind them were huge cooking pots—five feet across and two and a half feet deep—that were being used to cook "rice soup" (rice in water).

Cambodian people were chosen to cook, while the Khmer Rouge stood behind them with their guns. We did not know at this time that the soldiers would eat separately from us. They had good food: meat, rice, vegetables—everything.

The Khmer Rouge gave one bowl of rice soup to each person. There were thousands and thousands of people to be fed. I said to myself, *I could eat at least five or six bowls. I haven't eaten anything in the last twenty-four hours.*

The Khmer Rouge said that we had to stay right there tonight, and tomorrow we would walk a short way and then go to work. They pointed to where we would be working. I saw a river very far away.

The next morning, the Khmer Rouge said, "Wake up, let's get to work."

They walked us closer to the river. Then they stopped us for another meeting. They said, "You will be digging and carrying dirt. You will dump the dirt into the water so it will block the water from coming through. We are going to build a dam so that we can have a road through the jungle."

I looked at the wide, deep river. I could barely see the people in white on the other side. The Khmer Rouge told everybody, "Your equipment cannot be repaired or fixed when we are working. If you break your equipment, then you will be taken away and sent to a meeting."

We did not know at that time that the "meeting" meant you would be taken away and killed.

6 The Dam

I was captured in April 1975. Three weeks later, we all—several thousand people—were organized to work on building a dam on a river, the name of which I cannot recall. We were forced to work around the clock, twenty-three hours a day, with one hour to lie down and rest. We were fed one bowl of rice soup a day. We were given only a five-minute break to eat. We dug with our shovels and then poured the dirt into the twin buckets. Each bucket would hold about twenty-five pounds of dirt. When they were full, we put the bamboo pole across our shoulders and walked over to the river.

The river was huge and moving fast. The water was full of fish, snakes, and crocodiles. Fortunately, no one was hurt by snakes or crocodiles. There were so many people there making noise that the snakes were chased away. The Khmer Rouge did not plan on using wood or rock for a structure. We were simply going to pour dirt into the rushing water until a dam of earth was formed.

I approached the river with my heavy twin buckets. I could barely see thousands and thousands of white shirts on the other side, carrying their buckets to the river. When I got to the bank and dumped my dirt into the water, it just swirled away. It looked like I had dumped some milk into the brown water.

After two weeks straight, with no sign that any of the dirt was doing more than washing away, many people became fed up with the horrible work and started breaking their equipment, thinking this would get them out of working. The Khmer Rouge came to these workers and told them to go to a "freedom meeting" over in the jungle. The rest of us kept working.

Later, when I took a break, I went over to the jungle to see for myself what the "freedom meeting" was about. There, in the jungle, were the dead bodies of the workers who had broken their shovels and buckets. The workers had tried to fix their equipment, but Khmer Rouge soldiers took them away and beat them to death. Some of the dead workers had been my friends.

We worked like that, week after week and month after month, at the same place. At first, when we carried the dirt to the river, the riverbank was really close. But as we kept digging, the hole from which we got the dirt for the dam got deeper and farther away. Soon the hole was so far away that we had to walk down into the hole in lines to get to the fresh dirt. After we filled our buckets, we then walked up a steep bank, at least two hundred feet high, carrying our fifty-pound loads.

Thousands of people did this around the clock. I would get dizzy from looking at the people and then at the Khmer Rouge, standing over us with their guns. Dressed in good clothes and rain gear, they rotated in shifts. Thousands of soldiers watched our every move. Anyone who did anything wrong was taken away to the jungle.

At night, the work area was lit by small light bulbs. The electricity came from a generator driven by the river.

At first the people sang and walked with energy. After two months, there was no more singing. People walked slowly, with their heads down.

We started the dam in May and were still working around the clock in August, when the monsoons started. The rain in Cambodia during monsoon season is very heavy and nonstop. It rained every hour of the day and night. The dirt was now a sea of mud, and we had to climb up the steep bank, barefoot, while packing the heavy buckets, which was nearly impossible. People were slipping and sliding, always falling down into other people. If you fell down, it was hard to get back up. The Khmer Rouge would scream at us to wake up.

We were getting weaker, but the Khmer Rouge kept yelling at us to work harder. I knew I needed food or I would soon die.

I estimated that five thousand people already had died of starvation since we arrived at this terrible work place. Every day, people would fall down and not be able to get up. If they could not get up, they were hauled away and tossed in dump trucks with living and dead bodies.

Every day, these trucks waited next to us for those who could not work. By now we knew where the dump trucks took these people. Large holes had been created by bombs (the Khmer Rouge did not like to use shovels). The trucks drove away, backed up to these holes, and dumped the dead and living into a common grave.

As the dam grew bigger and the river got smaller, the water rose and rushed faster and faster, taking away the dirt from the sides of the dam.

I had been working for about eight months (this is an estimate because I kept time by the sun and memory; there were no watches or calendars). My clothes were rotting off my body. This was all I had to wear, so I had to be careful not to tear the clothes even more.

I looked down at my body and could see that I was nothing but skin and bones. My knees nearly poked through my skin, and my legs were as small as my arms used to be. I was used to having big muscles from doing tae kwon do, but now I could barely keep walking. When I looked at my friends, I saw their eyes were sunken in their faces—just black holes and skin and bones staring back at me.

7 | *The Flood*

One day in August 1975, a huge black cloud came over us, and the rain fell stronger than ever. Suddenly, the wall of dirt in the river began to collapse. Thousands of people were near or below the wall. I was halfway up the wall, getting ready to dump my load of dirt, when the part below me collapsed and rushed off to bury anything in its path. Below me, I saw a thousand people disappear under the brown mud. I hung onto the trees and shrubs on the riverbank, trying not to slip down. I was afraid that my life was about over.

The water behind the dam, which had been rising every day, suddenly knocked the dam completely away and rushed off, carrying workers and all the dirt we had poured into the water. Even the Khmer Rouge were killed in this moment.

The water swept people away so fast that they had no chance to escape or be rescued. There was no way to swim for shore. Anyone caught in the water was drowned. In a single minute, over a thousand people lost their lives.

I could do nothing to help anyone. I could not move for fear of falling into the water. I just sat, shaking in horror at the sight. All the work we had done for eight months was washed away. The river now looked just as it had when we first arrived.

The mud on the side of the dam had rushed down on top of the workers. Most had no warning and were buried alive in an instant.

In one second, they were trying to climb the bank of mud, and in the next, they were dead. The scene was horrible, with those of us who were alive screaming in horror.

The Khmer Rouge did not know what to do and began yelling at us to start digging out the buried people. Many of their soldiers were caught in the collapsed dirt. We began to dig, but so many workers were now gone that we could not dig the people out very fast.

A half hour later, the Khmer Rouge arrived with more workers. We did not know where they'd come from. These people were ordered to go down into the hole and dig the dirt out. Like me, they were very afraid. As they dug in the dirt, they struck the newly dead bodies. These were pulled out and tossed in dump trucks.

Once again, there were no girls in this new crew. When I looked at the new group of young boys, I saw they were starved—everyone was just skin and bones.

The Khmer Rouge were very angry with us after the water washed the dam away. Their faces were red and distorted. They struck out at everyone near them, hitting them with the butts of their rifles. They had lost many soldiers, and they blamed us for this, even though we had done nothing wrong. We had worked hard, every hour of every day, never letting up. No food, no sleep. But they were angry with us just the same.

That day was one of the worst days around the Khmer Rouge. If anyone did something out of line or said anything, the soldiers would take him out and beat him to death. We just put our heads down and worked.

Later that day, some of the Khmer Rouge were crying over the death of their soldiers. For their dead, they made us dig graves and create neat mounds for the graves. Meanwhile, our dead were being thrown in trucks and hauled off to be tossed in bomb holes.

This made me angry. It was our custom to burn our dead so their spirits could be released. A buried body could not let its spirit go; its ghost would walk in this terrible place forever.

I watched the Khmer Rouge crying and yelling at us to dig more graves for their dead. I wanted to fight them, but there was nothing I could do. They had guns. They were strong. All I could do was pray for help to come.

Each day, I worked like this. I worked and prayed every day, all day, in each moment. I prayed to God, to all the angels, and to everyone, living or dead, who ever knew me to please come help me.

There was no way to escape the Khmer Rouge. There were so many of them, always watching us. They worked in shifts so that we would never be left alone. There was no way to stop the endless work. Stop working, and you were dead.

As I grew more tired, my brain began to deaden. I no longer thought of my family. All I thought of was that one scoop of rice and salt and being careful with my equipment, so that I would not be sent to a "freedom meeting."

I was always hungry but could not say anything about this to the other workers. If the Khmer Rouge heard you complain, you were taken away. When I saw friends, all we could talk about was work. We had to be very careful of what we said around the Khmer Rouge, so we would say things like, "If we work hard, we will get more food."

This would make the soldiers smile.

8 The Rice Fields

One morning in September 1976, a Khmer Rouge soldier called us together. He said, "We have a new job for you," but he never said what it was. That scared me. I asked my friend, "What kind of job? Are we dead or alive?" The Khmer Rouge told the crew to set our equipment on a dump truck and then told us to climb on the truck.

In that minute, I told myself, "I am dead." I thought maybe they would dump me somewhere. We all prayed. I prayed to Mom and Dad, Grandma and Grandpa, and anyone who had ever loved me to help so that they wouldn't dump us somewhere. I looked at everyone's faces in the line; they were ghost faces, like they were already dead. In that moment, I missed my parents and family.

We walked over to the truck. I stood there, realizing I did not have the strength to climb up into the truck. When I was in school and did tae kwon do, I could jump and kick very high. But on this day, I was so weak that my friends had to help lift me into the steel truck. The steel hurt my bones as I fell in.

Our crew sat together, talking in soft voices. I wondered where they were taking us and what we had done wrong. We all were sure we were dead. I kept thinking of the people who had been washed away in the flood. If I closed my eyes, the images of the mud and the bodies filled my thoughts.

I looked at the Khmer Rouge standing around us; they were

smiling and farting. It smelled bad from their eating lots of good food. They pointed at us and told us to sit on the benches on the sides of the truck. They lined up and pointed their guns down at us.

At that moment, I was sure I was dead but did not know what to do. I could not talk to my crew, so I talked to myself. If I jumped out of the truck and ran, I was dead. If I stayed in the truck, I was dead—people in the trucks were always dumped in a big hole.

We drove away, bumping and bouncing in the back of the truck. We had to hold onto each other to keep from falling out. As we traveled, I prayed for everybody; I just prayed, prayed, and prayed.

After two hours, the truck left the jungle and came out into the fields, where it stopped. I saw huge rice fields, so large that I could not see the end of them. The truck pulled up alongside one of the fields, where at least twenty dump trucks were in a long line. The Khmer Rouge stopped our truck and said we were taking a break.

I was very scared. I thought we were about to be killed. There was a whole bunch of Khmer Rouge waiting for us with guns. I started to cry but no tears would come from my eyes. We were told to get out and go over to some people who were in a field. I thought there would be a large hole there.

I told my people, "This is my day to die. It is our day to die. When we die, we will all die together. We are done on this earth today. We will soon be in the sky."

We walked up to the Khmer Rouge. They asked us how we were doing, and we replied, "We are happy."

They answered, "Good," and told us to line up. Now I knew we were dead. Four or five soldiers came up and one said, "Do you know why you are here?"

"No."

"You are here to work this field."

I was so relieved that I told my friend in a soft voice, "Hey! This is our new job. Cool!"

We gathered so the Khmer Rouge could tell us what to do in our new job. We were glad to be here now because our old job of digging dirt was very hard. For a moment, there was a feeling of relief. Then they told us to pile up our equipment, and I thought, *Oh-oh, something is wrong. Maybe this was just a trick.*

They pointed and said, "See that dump truck over there? It hauls something."

They didn't say what that "something" was. Then all the crews walked toward the field. We were all barefoot and without hats. It was a half-hour walk to the field. The jungle had been cool, but the field was hot.

The grass was sharp and cut our feet. We had to scrunch up our toes and push the grass down as we walked. This way the grass bent over instead of cutting our feet to shreds. While we walked like this, the line of trucks waited for us at the side of the field.

That evening the Khmer Rouge gave us rice soup with a very small amount of rice; we could hardly see the rice in it. We also got our chunk of rock salt. We threw our bowls to the side of the road for the Khmer Rouge to collect. Soon there were big blue flies everywhere, sticking to the bowls. We slept on the dirt floor of the jungle next to the field. The Khmer Rouge slept in hammocks with rain gear to protect them. It rained hard that night, so we slept together, with our heads together, trying to stay warm. We talked among ourselves that night about the dam breaking, the people dying, the cold, and the wet. We were sleeping on the edge of the rice fields. The water was warm, but we were soaked all night.

9 *The Ghost Fields*

We were awakened at six in the morning and got no breakfast. There was no set time for getting up. Some mornings it was five o'clock, and other days it was seven—whenever the Khmer Rouge decided. We didn't refuse. We were split into many crews and into many different fields. There must have been a thousand people. Each rice paddy was one hundred meters by one hundred meters and surrounded by a bank of dirt. The Khmer Rouge walked around on dirt trails. They told us the fields needed to be cleaned up. I thought, *This will be good. We will finally have fresh air.*

My crew of thirty walked to a rice field, and the Khmer Rouge told us we would soon be planting rice, but first we had to clean all the junk and debris in the field, left there after flooding. I looked out into the field and could see the white clothes of workers already out there.

We started cleaning. At first, it was easy. We picked up sticks and wood, but then I saw something that was not right. As we walked out into the field, I realized that the people in white were dead bodies floating in the water. Some were face down; some were on their backs.

The Khmer Rouge shouted from the side of the field, telling us to pick up the bodies and put them in the dump truck. We looked around us and noticed that the field was full of white bodies covered with blue flies.

I told my friend, "You pick them up!"

"No! You pick them up."

The Khmer Rouge yelled, "All you guys pick them up—help pick them up!"

We tried to pick up the bodies, but they were heavy and swollen. We tried to move them, but we couldn't. We had no strength, no energy to do it.

One kid next to us grabbed an arm to try to move the body. He pulled and pulled as hard as he could. Suddenly, the arm came off in his hands. The kid fell over and splashed into the water holding the arm.

Another kid tried to pull a body by its leg. The leg came off, and he also fell down.

My friend and I went over to a body. We each grabbed a hand so that we could drag the body away. As we pulled on the arms, they both came off the body. I thought I would be sick. I looked up at the Khmer Rouge, who were looking at me. I acted like I was fine.

Two more from my crew grabbed the dead body's legs and they came off. The four of us stood there holding pieces of the dead body. The Khmer Rouge yelled at us to bring the pieces to the truck. They had nose plugs for the horrible smell.

Each body that we moved came apart in pieces. The work was so awful that many of my crew fell down from dizziness. We tried to help them up, but the Khmer Rouge yelled at us not to help those who fell down.

The field was swarming with thousands and thousands of fat blue flies. The blue flies were fat from eating on the bodies, and they would land on our bare heads to rest. We moved bodies like this for six straight hours. The bodies looked hideous—black circles around their eyes, bellies swollen, and pieces of flesh falling off. Finally, the Khmer Rouge told us to take a break.

We walked over to a small hillock, and I noticed small frogs jumping on the bank. I caught one and tucked it in the fold of my pants. I would eat it later that night. If we ate in front of the Khmer Rouge, they would kill us.

After a short rest we were told to go back to work. My clothes were soaked and filthy from working in the water all day. As we cleaned the field, I noticed that some of the dead people had much better clothes than I had. Many of the shirts and pants were in good shape. I wanted to swap their clothes for mine, but we could not do this either. The Khmer Rouge were everywhere. I told my friend that the shirt on the dead body was very good, while mine was terrible and ripped.

My friend told me, "Don't take it. Don't wear that shirt or the Khmer Rouge will kill you."

We cleaned up field after field. When we took a break at six in the evening, we figured we had cleaned away about six hundred dead bodies, and we still were not done. I looked over at the other fields and noticed that crews were finding bodies in every other rice field. Each of the fields was the same, with muddy, yellowish-green water surrounded by dirt, where the Khmer Rouge stood with guns.

We were thirsty and had to drink the dirty water from those fields. I held my shirt over the surface of the water and sucked through it. Some crew members were too tired and brokenhearted to pick up the bodies anymore. If someone fell in the field, the Khmer Rouge said, "Just put that one in the truck, too."

We would try to stand him up, but if he fell again, he was ordered to be taken out. The Khmer Rouge would stand on the dry bank of dirt, yelling at us to carry our friend out of the rice field. We had to carry him and then dump him in the truck, still alive, with the dead bodies.

10 *Hanging in There*

Each day we did this terrible work. Somehow, I became used to standing with the dead bodies and sleeping next to them at night. When we threw the bodies in the trucks, I talked to them nicely, saying, "Good-bye. You go first, and I go last. I don't know when."

How many thousands of dead had wound up in these fields? We did not know, but my crew picked up eighteen hundred bodies in five days. There were over one hundred dump trucks standing by the field.

On the fifth night, the Khmer Rouge called us to eat and told us that the total count for all crews had been forty-five hundred people. We couldn't ask why; nobody asked the Khmer Rouge anything.

We still had thirty workers left in my crew. One crew had only fifteen left. These people could no longer walk or clean the field. We could not help them. The Khmer Rouge took these fifteen away to dump them somewhere.

They announced to us that if anybody got sick, we were not to help them. "Do not touch them."

The Khmer Rouge told us they would handle it. They let us know that if we got sick and couldn't work, we were gone. Then they told us to go eat, so we went to the side of the field and ate our one bowl of rice soup. Then we went to sleep right there, next to the water, for the night.

That night, I talked with my friend. I asked him how he was doing. He said, "Not good."

I told him, "Hang in there. In a few days, we will go somewhere else."

"It's no good," he said. "It's too stinky, walking around the dead people."

"I stink too," I responded. "You eat rice soup. I eat rice soup. I drink water in the field like you. I sleep next to dead bodies in wet clothes. Hang in there. Pray that someone will come to help us. We don't know who or when, but they will come." I told him that it was good for us to help clean up the dead people, that maybe it was somebody's brother or sister.

The next morning, the Khmer Rouge took us to another place, and we saw many big blue flies. My friend walked ahead of me and saw the reason for all the swarming blue flies. There was a big hole with sixty to a hundred people piled up in it. All their clothes were different, not white.

While I stood looking in the hole, the Khmer Rouge called my crew together. I ran for the back of the line. I was scared to death. If they saw me looking in the hole, I was dead.

They started calling out our names. I was supposed to be standing in the middle of the line. When they got to my name, I shouted from the back of the line that I was at the end. The Khmer Rouge then called the next name. I was still alive.

We went to work, cleaning up the field some more. They told us that all the fields needed to be finished. If the fields were not cleaned up today, we would be in trouble, so we kept working. Everyone in my crew worked as hard as they could in the mud, flies, and heat to get the last bodies out of the field. Some of my crew could barely walk. Some were very sick and dizzy, only a day away from the truck themselves.

* * *

On that day in 1976, I was sixteen years old. I had already survived one year in the Killing Fields. With my young eyes, I had seen all kinds of terrible things. I slept with dead people and then made them my friends. I drank the water where they lay.

I told myself that if I didn't die like those people, then I had to go forward. I thought about my future, and I kept praying. At every corner of the field, I prayed that someone would come down and help me and my friends get out of this horrible place and get to freedom. We all prayed like this, all day, every day.

On that last day of cleaning up the dead bodies, I thought about my teacher in school, how he had said to always do good things for all people. I had listened to his words. I told myself that maybe I had done good things in my life before this. Maybe that was why I was still alive. Maybe if I hadn't done good things, I would have been dead already.

I prayed to Buddha and to everyone to whom I had been good. I prayed that I would not be stuck in the mud and the green/brown water of these fields until I was dead.

My eyes were now big holes. I could see my bones and my ribs. When I sat down that night, my knees were on my ears.

I looked at the Khmer Rouge, laughing and playing games in their shelters. They were strong, slept a lot, and ate all kinds of good food.

I thought to myself, *They will never die*.

11 *The Sound of Death*

The morning after our project was completed (sometime in October 1977), I saw that the field we had just cleaned had turned green with bundles of rice. They were everywhere. I wondered how this had happened. We did not know that another crew had worked during the night, filling the field with bundles. The Khmer Rouge called us together and said that the field was now ready for planting. They then taught us how to plant rice. Our job was to go out and break the bundles and then plant each individual rice stalk in the mud. We were to plant them as we walked backward through the field. We were trained to poke the rice plant in the field with our thumbs.

Out into the water we went. Soon, we found that stooping, planting, and walking backward in the heat, brown water, and mud was terrible. We all became very dizzy, which was dangerous, because if we fell down and couldn't get back up, we would be taken away.

Some people had never planted rice and did it wrong. If they poked the plants in wrong, the plants would not stay in the ground and would float on the water. The Khmer Rouge said that the people who did not plant correctly must not like freedom. If they planted too many wrong, they were gone. I was one of the people who had never planted rice, so I had to be very careful not to make a mistake.

Before we started planting the fields, I had thought that removing the dead bodies was the worst work. As it turned out, planting the rice fields was even worse. I took each plant out of the large bundle, stuck it down in the mud, and then scooped through the mud with my thumb. Bent over in the thick heat, with the smell of dead bodies in the air, it was hard to keep from getting sick.

We walked backward all day, planting in triangle patterns. Those who made the mistake of planting in a straight line were taken away. My crew had eight people who did not know how to plant. The Khmer Rouge pointed and asked, "Why do you plant like that?"

My friends each said, "I have never planted before."

The Khmer Rouge said, "You had a lesson, so why are the rice plants floating? You waste food. You have to plant close to the ground."

They took eight away that day. I could not say good-bye. Nothing. I never saw these friends again.

I watched how people planted the rice. Some fell down as they walked backward. Some people stood up after planting for hours and were so dizzy that they passed out and fell in the water.

The Khmer Rouge ran on the bank above us and shouted at those who fell. When the workers tried to get back up, they looked like drunk people. Their friends tried to pick them up and carry them when they fell. Some of the people just fell back down again.

The Khmer Rouge did not want us helping each other. They screamed to get away from the fallen. They called some of their crew over to take away the people who had tried to help. Later that day, four Khmer Rouge picked up the people who had fallen and dragged them out to the road and then to the jungle. That day, I saw them drag away fifteen to twenty people.

My friend Saron and I worked hard to make sure everything was right with us. As I walked backward, planting, I thought about those poor people, and I became dizzy. I almost fell, but my friend came over and held me up. He asked me what happened. I told him I was dizzy and could not see clearly. He said, "Don't think about anything. Just take care of yourself."

"It's not right," I said. "Some people have no experience planting."

To keep time, I watched the sun move that day and figured out that the Khmer Rouge took three to four people away every hour.

I told myself, "Hang in there. Tomorrow I will be dead, but now I am still alive."

I told my friend, "The people who were taken away were not lucky. You help me, and I'll help you. If I fall, help me up. We need to pray to all kinds—to the jungle, to Mom and Dad, to animals, to everything—to come help us. We have no food to eat, just the brown water to drink from the field. If you see something come close to you in the water, catch it and eat it."

From then on, if a fly landed on our faces, we ate it. Sometimes we were lucky and found a fish. These we tucked in our pants' folds to be eaten later, in the dark. Some nights, I would share a finger-sized fish with my friend.

We kept working in the field all day, every day, no matter how cold or hot the weather. We had no spare clothes. We were still in the white uniforms they had given us, but at this point, the clothes were rags. If the clothes got too bad, the Khmer Rouge would give us replacements, telling us to be more careful. Not only were my clothes becoming rags, but my hair was falling out. I was completely bald. This happened to everybody on my crew. We looked like monks. In one sense, we acted like monks. We prayed all day for rain because the Khmer Rouge ran away when it rained, and we could take a break, standing in the field. We were never allowed to sit.

The rain was sometimes very heavy. If the water got too deep to see the rice plant, which was about nine inches tall, we couldn't plant. Then we were happy.

One day, the Khmer Rouge called everybody to a meeting. They said, "Does anybody want to go to their hometown?"

We all said, "Yes, we want to go home."

They asked us if anybody was hungry.

We said we were.

They laughed at us. "Then what are you going to do about that?"

This taunting made me very angry. I wished I could kill them.

The Khmer Rouge said that we were there to plant rice and build dams to water the fields. They said that if we did this and got everything done, then we would go home and have freedom.

That day, I asked a Khmer Rouge if I could ask a question, and he said yes. My friend and I whispered to each other. I said to my friend, "Should I ask him about getting more food to eat?"

My friend said, "If you ask, he might kill you."

The Khmer Rouge said to me, "What is your question? Speak up fast!"

I asked if I could have more food for my crew.

He asked, "What food?"

"Rice," I answered. "We have been eating rice soup all the time, no meat."

"You want to eat rice? How can you get it? You just planted rice. You will have to wait three more months until it grows and has a seed."

That night it rained, and the Khmer Rouge said the water was too high. We were to take a break until the water went down. That day, all the crews rested.

Each crew was watched by a different group of Khmer Rouge. I kept thinking about what we could do. We were in the middle of the jungle. None of us knew how to get out. We knew that we would be food for the animals if we tried to run away.

Some of the Khmer Rouge were nicer to us than others. Some of them ate people's lungs.

One day, I was walking backward in the dark and dirty water. I took a step back and fell over something in the water. Under my legs was a dead body. This scared me.

The Khmer Rouge asked me what was wrong, but I told them I was okay. They told my crew to pick up the body and take it to the truck. Four of us carried the body to the truck. This one was freshly dead and didn't come apart when we picked it up.

My heart felt heavy and sick that day. Why had this person been killed? The sense of hopelessness made my heart sink like a stone. That night, I lay thinking that I could not keep doing this, that I would probably be dead the next day.

That week I made a new friend and carefully taught him how to plant the rice and catch food. At night, we talked and shared the small fish we caught and hid in our pants. This kept us alive.

One day, my friend planted a rice plant incorrectly. When he stuck the plant in the mud, he didn't pack the bottom tightly around the plant. The rice plant fell over in the water.

The Khmer Rouge said to him, "You do not like working here because your plant cannot stick on the ground!"

They took him away, telling him he was not worth it and that he was wasting the rice plants. As they pulled him from the field, he looked back at me. His face seemed to say, "Bun, I am dead." I could do nothing for him. He was my friend, and now he was gone.

My heart dropped that day. This was wrong. Everything was wrong. There was nothing I could do. The Khmer Rouge watched us every minute. There was no way to escape.

I planted hard that day, making sure the rice plant was firm. Since there was nothing I could do for anyone, I just took care of myself, working hard, and always wondering how much longer my life would last.

When I looked up, the Khmer Rouge were taking more people away from the field. I put my face down and planted again.

I prayed for help. I wondered how I could get out. I knew I was far from the city. I had never been in the jungle alone. I knew I would get lost and never find my way home.

That night, when I took my soup break, I could hear the animals of the jungle making their noises. The monkeys were chattering. The birds were singing. I talked with them that night. They were free. I thanked them for their freedom. The sound of their voices singing and talking gave me a bit of hope. I could see monkeys jumping in the trees. There were colorful birds, big and small. They were free. There had to be a way out of this place.

From sunrise until sunset, we planted in the field. Each day the temperature was over one hundred degrees. The air was so hot that plants not touched by water turned dry. If you rubbed them in your hands, they would turn to dust.

Because of the intense sun, the Khmer Rouge had large hats to protect their heads from the heat and flies. They would watch us for one hour, and then they were relieved and went to sit in the shade.

My crew worked in the fields with bare heads, bare hands, and bare feet—no protection from the tropical heat all day. We were always thirsty and had to drink the water lying in the field. There was no other water. I was afraid of getting sick, but I never did. I thought about the river and the dam and wanted to go back to digging dirt again.

All day in the field, I could hear a buzzing sound in my ear. When I plugged my ears it was gone. When I took my hand away, the buzzing came back. The people around me told me that the buzzing was the sound of death. They told me I would be dead soon.

I already knew this. I had no energy left in my body. My arms and legs were just skin and bones. I needed more food, or I would be gone, but how? I couldn't walk out of the field to the jungle, because the Khmer Rouge watched us twenty-four hours a day to make sure we didn't run away.

That night, we slept in the dirt on the side of the field. The grass next to us was filled with grasshoppers. I ate as many as I could catch.

"Good medicine," I told a new friend. We laughed and ate the grasshoppers together. I told him the grasshoppers would kill all the germs and evil things in the bad water.

One day, this new friend said he had a bad headache and wanted to sleep. I said, "Don't sit down. The Khmer Rouge is watching you. He might take you away."

My friend said he had such a bad headache that he couldn't stand up anymore. He just wanted to lie down. Before long, he lay down on the field. I tried to stand over him so the Khmer Rouge could not see him. It wasn't long before the Khmer Rouge called over to say, "Why is it taking so long to finish this field?"

Then he walked over to where my friend was and saw him down in the water in the field. He asked him why he wasn't working and what was wrong. My friend said his head hurt. The Khmer Rouge asked him, "You have a headache?"

"Yes, really bad."

Then the Khmer Rouge took him out of the field. To myself, I screamed, *I tried to help you, but they saw you! We just talked together last night, and today you are gone!*

That day, my crew finished the field. Then a storm came again, with black clouds and dark, heavy rain. The Khmer Rouge called us out to line up and eat. After we ate, they told us to go back in the field.

I wondered, *How can I plant in the heavy rain?*

I stood at the side of the field and watched the rain fall. My clothes were soaking wet, dripping with water. I looked at the Khmer Rouge, sitting under the roof of their house. Then they called to us, "You all come back and sleep here for another night."

That night, we slept under trees in the jungle, not in the field. The Khmer Rouge said that when we slept, we couldn't talk. If they heard us talking, we'd have trouble.

On that night, no one talked. We were all cold and wet, but we went to sleep. The Khmer Rouge stood by so we didn't run away. I asked myself, *What can they be thinking? How can I run? I have no energy. I have no idea where to go.*

The next morning, they said that they needed to finish the rice fields right now. We were to get it done today. That day, one thousand people worked together until dark to finish on time.

As the Khmer Rouge walked around our sleeping place, they said, "You'll be working on something different tomorrow." We had no idea what that meant—work or death.

12   *Dig Dirt, Bury Water*

With the field now planted, the Khmer Rouge told us we would be going back to the dam to start digging dirt again. I was very happy. This would be better for me. We were rounded up, put in trucks, and driven four hours back to the river. The road was very bumpy, and the trucks were slow. We could have walked faster, but no one wanted to walk.

That day, we didn't have to work. I talked with my crew about the field, carrying the dead, planting, the friends being taken away for not planting correctly, and workers being taken away after falling down.

We all looked forward to going back to the dam, because it was easy work for us. We just had to dig and lift dirt all day long. As long as we didn't break our equipment, we could do nothing wrong. We talked like this all day. It was my first day without work in nine months. The next morning when we awoke, we received new equipment. The fifteen people missing from our crew were replaced by another fifteen. We were told to walk a half mile to the dam.

In the distance, I could see the people working; they were walking slowly. The people looked at us as we approached. I said hello to them and told them we were new friends. They said nothing. Their faces just stared at us, like they were the walking dead. This scared me.

The river was huge, just like before. The dirt we poured in just floated away. The people we joined had been working like this for a year. None of their work had accomplished anything. The dam reached four hundred feet into the river, but the gap between the two parts of the dam was even wider. These workers had lost friends and all hope. Now, they just walked with their buckets of dirt, waiting for death.

I stepped in line and started digging again. Dig dirt, carry dirt, dump dirt, bury water. My friends and I took turns digging or carrying the dirt. Some dug, some carried. This gave us a change and a chance to take a break. We did this for twenty-three hours a day. There was no sick leave or vacation. "Vacation" meant they took you away to "freedom."

On that first day, I had thirty people in my crew. Each day after that, some of my friends died—death, death, death, every day, until I had only seven left. Then the Khmer Rouge took us seven to another crew, where five had died. We came together to make one crew. The new crew was terrible; they were skinny and hungry. I wanted to cry, but when I did, no tears came out.

One of the new crew took his clothes off, and I could see that he was really skinny, just like me. We were both just skin and bones. I said to him, "Hey, look at me! I am as skinny as you. So do you eat a lot?"

"Yeah. We eat one whole bowl of rice soup and one piece of salt a day," he answered sarcastically.

I took off my shirt and laughed. "Look at me! I am the same as you. You are like my brother!"

We laughed together, and then we prayed together. We talked about wanting to fight the Khmer Rouge, but they had guns, so we couldn't. They also had strength, unlike us. If the wind blew on me, I would fall over. When that happened, I had to get up really fast, before the Khmer Rouge dragged me away.

Our new crew slept on limbs of trees that we put on the ground, because if we slept close to the dirt, when we woke up, we would have no vitality.

My crew all became good friends. We helped each other, worked together, sang together, played together, and tried to forget about being hungry together.

We talked only about working, never about missing home or our mothers, fathers, brothers, or sisters—we didn't talk that way. The Khmer Rouge liked it when we talked about working hard and fast.

We kept digging the dirt around the clock. What hair I had left fell out during this time. All of my friends looked like this. We made a joke of this, saying that we all looked like newborn babies. We joked like this all day, singing songs, making our friends laugh, and trying not to think about our hungry bodies. We turned the work into play. We tried to make the best of our lives until we were dead.

Sometimes, I was so tired that I would close my eyes as I walked. I would come awake when I bumped into the person in front of me.

One year passed like this. People grew more and more hungry and tired. Some of my friends said they didn't have enough energy to carry the dirt and dump the dirt into the water. When this happened, they would die.

Some people couldn't walk anymore; they simply fell on the ground. I tried to help them, but the Khmer Rouge told me not to do that. "When you work, you keep working."

They said they had a person who would take care of the person on the ground. We knew what that meant.

The people started getting sick. The Khmer Rouge told them, "You are lazy, because you don't want to go to work." They threatened, "We have a place for people who get sick."

One day, I saw a friend in front of me with his equipment broken. Then I saw the Khmer Rouge run to him. The Khmer Rouge asked what happened, and he said his equipment broke. They told him he was done working for today, and two Khmer Rouge came to get him. I saw where they took him. Not far away, they beat him to death with a large stick. This was how they were killing us now—beating us to death to save the bullets in their guns.

That day as we ate our soup, a Khmer Rouge soldier screamed, "Anybody who breaks their equipment will not have any more questions to ask!"

At the end of that day, the Khmer Rouge got us up early the following morning, so I could look forward to another early start the next day. It wasn't long after we started work the next morning that we got heavy rain. We couldn't see clearly because the rain was coming down in sheets. Water poured off my head and clothes.

When I went to sleep that night, my clothes still were wet. We slept out on the ground with no roofs. I was very cold. I started to pray, "Buddha, ancestors, Grandma, Grandpa, Mother, Father, all those people who passed away, come help me because I am so hungry and cold." I didn't know where my family was. I wondered if they were doing the same terrible work as me.

As usual, the Khmer Rouge had a roof so they wouldn't get wet. They had food—meat and vegetables. They were laughing and playing games.

13 The Lucky Snake

By 1977, my crew began to look at the ground for food. Every time we went to relieve ourselves in the jungle, we would look for food. None of us ever had to poop, because there was nothing inside of us, so we would just fake needing to go so that we could look for something to eat. At this point, we were eating anything we could find. Sometimes we could find a tree that had fruit. It might be too high to reach, but sometimes a bird would eat a part of the fruit, and it might fall from the tree. Then we could find it and eat it.

One day my friend came back from going to pee; he looked excited. "I found a large python that has eaten an animal and cannot move. This snake is as big around as a tree! He has a lot of meat on him! We need to kill this snake to eat, but how can we kill him? We don't have a knife."

"Use anything around to kill it," I said. And this was one time when we had some good luck.

That day, my crew went out one at a time during our pee breaks to sneak over to the python and eat the raw meat. When it was my turn, I asked the Khmer Rouge if I could go to pee. Then I hurried away from the job, found a sharp stick, and ate the snake's meat.

I chewed the raw, bloody meat really fast, being careful not to spill blood on my clothes. After I was done, I washed up so there was no blood on my face and told my friend, "After you eat, clean yourself so there is no blood on your mouth."

After that, thirty more people ate meat from the snake. The last two kids who ate tried to eat too fast and came back with blood spilled on their white clothes. The Khmer Rouge asked them, "Where did the blood come from?"

One boy said, "I am hungry. I ate a snake."

The Khmer Rouge asked, "Where'd you get the snake?"

The kids told them where it was. The Khmer Rouge took those two kids away from our group.

The next morning, after I had worked for a while, I asked the Khmer Rouge if I could go pee—I wanted to eat some more meat. When I ran down there, I saw that the snake was gone, but the two kids' bodies were there, with their throats cut. I ran back to work and told my crew what I had seen. After that, I kept thinking, *How can I get food?*

That same day, I saw a lot of people lying on the ground. The Khmer Rouge had dragged them away because they could not work anymore.

Later that day, people were leaning on the trees, breathing very slowly. I shook one of them awake and asked, "How are you?" When he didn't say anything, I said, "Whoa, you are almost dead." I didn't know if he was going to last another minute.

When I walked away from those people, the wind blew me off the road, and I fell but then got back up quickly before the Khmer Rouge could see me.

Every day, I saw people who couldn't stand up being taken away. Every hour, every minute, the people kept working around the clock until they collapsed.

There was nothing left on my body—no muscle, no fat. I was just a walking skeleton. But I kept going.

Then one day, the Khmer Rouge announced on the big speakers, "All the people here right now who are still alive will continue to work until we are done building this dam. All those people who are dead are the people who are lazy. Those kids made no difference for anything. If they are dead and gone, no problem."

This made me very angry. I wished I could fight the Khmer Rouge. I wanted to kill them. To say that those kids made no difference was an outrage.

14 No Food for Animals

The next morning, the Khmer Rouge told us that we were going back to cut the rice we had planted. It was close to wintertime, and the rain had slowed down. We got in the trucks and headed back to the rice fields.

We were all given sickle knives and were taught how to walk through the dry fields, cutting and binding the rice plants. This was a better time for me. The fields were dry. We were always walking forward, so I didn't get dizzy. Better, the plants hid mice and rats and grasshoppers.

When we caught a mouse, we snapped its neck and then hid it in our clothes. Doing this, we would eat one or two a day. We had to be very careful, eating this food. We could never be seen with anything in our mouths, or we would be dead.

During this time, my friend taught me how to kill a rat, skin it with my fingers, and squeeze the blood off into the water. This way, we had fresh white meat with no blood. No blood meant there was less chance of being caught eating. We learned to do this quickly.

For a month, we cut and bound the rice and walked it to a cart that was pulled by a bull. When the cart was full, we walked behind it for a half mile to another field. Then we emptied the cart, walked back to the field, and loaded up the cart again. We did this all day. This job was pleasant compared to the other work. The only problem was that the rice was very dry and made our legs itch.

One morning, the Khmer Rouge said, "All the rice is cut. You will come back to plant again after the fields are plowed. Now, you go back to your old job of carrying dirt and water."

I thought that both jobs were hard in different ways. I thought, *Just go to work day by day, week by week, month by month. Just stay alive. Don't think about anything.*

The next morning, we went to work at the old job. Same hard work. Same trouble. My life was simple. Dig dirt, plant rice, dig dirt again, cut rice. Day after day, week after week, month after month, year after year. Every second my body grew weaker. Every day I had to tell my body, "Hang in there."

All the workers talked about the rice we had just cut. We all hoped that we would get to eat more rice now. There were fields of rice. Plenty of rice for everyone. We had seen it. My friends told me that if we could eat a whole bowl of rice, we would have power for an entire week.

The days passed, but we never saw the rice. It never came. We had no idea what happened to that harvest.

After two years, I recognized only fifty or sixty people who had survived as long as I had. All of us were bald and skin and bones. When I would see one of these old friends, I would feel happy. We would tell one another, "We must have done good things. Our parents must have done good things."

We thought that Buddha must appreciate us and all the good we had done. I thought about how my mom used to go in the temple and help all the poor people. Maybe that was why I was still alive.

I kept working, even though I did not have enough to eat or enough sleep. We were angry with the Khmer Rouge because they never worked. They always had guns pointed at people, telling them to work faster. We could not fight back. We all just waited for one day, one week, one year when we would have freedom. We didn't know, however, when or if that day would ever come.

Another morning in 1977 came, and we lined up to go back to work, like we always did. That day, there were massive black clouds. Soon another big storm hit. The water in the river rose and poured over the dam, washing it away again. There was no rock or wood to hold the dirt in place. The dirt around us collapsed and thousands of people were buried again.

The Khmer Rouge again needed us to dig the dirt off those who had been buried alive. My crew went down to help. People dug around the clock, even in the dark. My crew of five dug by hand or used small shovels. People moved the dirt all day and all night. We would see a hand or leg and pull out a dead body.

The Khmer Rouge screamed at us over megaphones to dig faster. Some of their soldiers were buried in the dirt. When the people tried to dig really hard, some would collapse and die.

The Khmer Rouge kept yelling at us to keep digging. My friend dug dirt, and I carried buckets away. The Khmer Rouge told my friend to hurry up, so he tried to dig faster.

Then the Khmer Rouge brought about two hundred more people into the hole with my crew to try to dig out the dirt. The dirt collapsed again and hit us. Of the two hundred people, 170 were killed.

Now only thirty of us were left to do the digging and try to get the rest of the crew out. The Khmer Rouge saw that everyone was working very hard and brought a hundred of their soldiers to help us dig. With the help of the stronger Khmer Rouge, it did not take that long to get the bodies out. Side by side we dug, with the river water pouring in, and the rain water pouring down.

We all slipped around and fell in the mud. My crew was amazed by how fast the Khmer Rouge could work, compared to us. One hour later, we had all the bodies out of there.

That day, I figured at least two to three thousand people were either swept away or buried alive. The collapse of the dirt had happened in an instant. There was no warning. One moment there were thousands of people digging and dumping dirt; the next moment, they were gone. It looked like magic—poof! Just dirt and silence where thousands of crew had been standing an instant before.

Later that day, the Khmer Rouge brought in new people to replace the dead workers. These people had never experienced digging dirt.

My crew was finally brought out of the hole, because we were all very tired. The Khmer Rouge gave us one hour to take a break. I was very happy, because we had never had a break like that before. I tried looking for my group, but I found only seven out of the thirty. The rest were gone.

After the break, we started digging again. We put dead bodies into the dump trucks that sat waiting for us. I was so tired that I walked with my eyes closed. I told myself, "I don't care anymore. If I die, it is fine."

I had just lost my good friends for nothing. The Khmer Rouge didn't care about any of them. They cared about their crew and cried over the loss of their friends. It wasn't right. That day, I was ready to give up. I could barely pick up my legs. All of us were slow, exhausted, and defeated. We were all mad at the Khmer Rouge but could do nothing about it—nothing. There was no place to run. No way to get away from their guns. We were all too weak to escape very far into the jungle. Again we realized that we would just be food for the animals.

That night, I missed my friends. The night before, we had slept together and talked. Now, they were gone. I lay down and prayed to be taken from this place. Dead or alive. I didn't care anymore. There was nothing left of me. No hair, no muscle, no friends—nothing.

I laughed at myself. "If I die, an animal will see me, look at my body, and know there is nothing for him to eat. He will just walk up, smell my body, and walk away saying, 'Hey! You have no meat.' Poor animal, if you find me, you are not lucky."

15 The Uprising

The next morning, the Khmer Rouge called my crew over. They said they saw us working very hard and wanted us to show the new people how to work. They split us into three groups of ten. Ten of us were in charge of a thousand new workers. We showed them how to work and how to be careful. We trained them for five days, until they knew what they were doing.

We had fun together, digging the dirt. We worked day and night. As long as the power was on and the light was on, we had to keep working. Every day we prayed for the light to go off. Some of my crew grabbed rocks and broke the lights. Then we'd hear, "Okay, break time."

The Khmer Rouge would find a bulb and replace it. When the lights came on, we would applaud like we were happy to get back to work. But the Khmer Rouge knew we were happy to have gotten a break, so they guarded the lights.

The people's bodies kept getting smaller and smaller. Just skin and bones. They knew that they would be dead soon.

One day, the Khmer Rouge announced that it was the New Year 1978. On that day, they told us that anybody who wanted to go home had to work very fast, and then they could go to their hometown. They told us not to think about our old story, our old life, our old house, or our parents, brothers, or sisters. When this project was done, we would have a new life and see our parents again.

All of us workers came together to listen to this announcement; about ten thousand of us stood there. After that, all the people walked away. I said, "Shit, nobody believes the Khmer Rouge."

My friend told me, "Don't say bad words, Bun. The Khmer Rouge will hear you."

The next morning the Khmer Rouge called us to go to work. We worked for about half a day, but some people couldn't hang in there. They got mad about what the Khmer Rouge had said to us about working hard and going home. They picked up shovels to hit the Khmer Rouge next to them. Another group of Khmer Rouge raced in and shot them right there.

That night, I got mad and talked to the crew. I asked a friend if anyone had gotten hurt, and he said that a friend was shot in the face and died.

My friend said, "What can we do?"

"I'm not afraid to die anymore," I told him.

Of three thousand people working on the dam, we only had 150 left.

The new crew, which had come from a part of Cambodia where the conditions were not as bad as these, heard this. These people were very mad at the Khmer Rouge. They were not used to the terrible work we had at this dam. Very soon, the new crews got up, grabbed sticks, rocks, and their equipment, and went over to fight with the Khmer Rouge. They wanted to burn down the houses where the Khmer Rouge were sleeping.

The Khmer Rouge heard them coming, ran out, and started shooting them like animals. The people screamed loudly, "I'm not afraid to die anymore!"

In the dark, the Khmer Rouge didn't know who was who. They just emptied their guns into the people. When the gunfire stopped, at least 250 had been shot dead. Many others were still alive, with broken arms and legs.

When the next morning came, the Khmer Rouge called my crew out to clean up the bodies. "Put them over there on a dry spot for now," they said. We dragged the dead out of the houses and piled them up in one place. It did not take long.

After that, the Khmer Rouge tied about twenty grenades in a bundle and put them away from the house. Then they shot at the bundle to explode the grenades and make a big hole in the ground, as big as a pond. After the smoke was gone, they called us over to move the bodies of our friends into the hole. Some of them were still alive. They went in the hole too. We all had to do it, because if we did not, the Khmer Rouge would have killed us. As we tossed them in the hole, some of the people called out, "Help me! Help me!"

What could I do? I just dropped them in and walked away. These were my friends. I saw some with broken arms, broken legs, and blood everywhere. After this was done, my crew and I just prayed for them. "In your next life, may you have a good father, a good mother, and no more trouble like this."

We kept moving. All my crew kept moving. We had no energy left, but the Khmer Rouge kept screaming, "Hurry up! Hurry up!"

My crew couldn't say anything to them. Back home, we had been strong and could carry heavy weight. But now we were all so weak. It took four of us to move one dead body. We tried to help each other lift the bodies and keep from falling down.

I asked a Khmer Rouge, "Please, can you help the people who are not dead yet? Some are still alive."

But he answered, "No, we don't have any doctors." Then he took his gun, pointed it in the hole, and shot some of them again in the head. At that point, my heart flew away. The Khmer Rouge told me to go back to work. He said, "You want to help them? Then you will die too." That scared me. He yelled at me, "You want to go in the hole?"

I said, "No."

The Khmer Rouge walked one way, and my crew walked another way. When I looked back, the Khmer Rouge had jumped in a truck and gone away. My crew ran back to the hole to look at the people.

"I want to check on our people," I said.

My friend nodded. "I will watch for the Khmer Rouge while you sneak in."

I went down in the hole and looked at the people who were still alive. There were about 150 in there. I just looked at them with their shattered legs and arms, and I was scared. I asked myself, *How can I help? If I do anything, the Khmer Rouge will kill me too!*

The people in the hole were all moaning, "Help, help, help." It sounded like animals moaning. I walked on top of the bodies, knowing there was nothing we could do. I thought, *If you fight the Khmer Rouge, this is what happens.*

I looked at them. The ones who were dead were lucky. For those who were still alive in that hole, it was terrible. I wanted to cry, but no tears would come. I climbed out of the moaning bodies and said to myself, *We tried to do something to help them, but it didn't work; they couldn't walk. All those people will be dead tomorrow anyway.*

My clothes were soaked red. Only my back was white. My front was covered in blood from picking up the bodies.

I ran back to my crew and told my friend, "If we try to help them and the Khmer Rouge show up, we will be dead in the hole, just like them."

We talked for about fifteen minutes, trying to decide what to do. Then the Khmer Rouge came back. They asked us what we were doing, and we said we were taking a break. Five empty trucks arrived, and they told us to climb on. As the trucks took off, my friend said, "I don't know where we are going, but it's only one of two ways—either dead or alive."

I said, "Well, if they kill us, we are dead; if we are still in the truck and they drop us off, we are still alive."

We didn't talk after that. We were sitting in the back with the Khmer Rouge, who were afraid that we might jump out of the truck and escape into the jungle. They sat with us even though we were too tired to run anywhere. We were too tired to even talk.

They dropped us off at a field and told us to follow them. It was almost night.

I said to myself, "This is the last time I am alive." Then I told my friend, "We are dead now." We tried to cry, but it did not work. Our bodies were too dry.

We walked and heard some people screaming and yelling, "Help, help!"

This scared us even more. I said, "This is the last day for us!"

All of my crew listened to the people screaming for help. We were all so scared! It was like our spirits were connected to our bodies by only one last hair.

We kept walking. When I heard the screams, I thought about the past. I thought about loading bodies in the trucks and those people screaming as they were tossed in on top of the dead bodies.

We were scared to death as we followed the Khmer Rouge. We still had no idea where they were taking us. Later that night, we took a break, and they cooked for us. My friends and I looked at each other. We were still alive. We were all teenage boys, living in the jungle, pulling dead bodies out of dirt, drinking bad water every day, and sleeping in soaking-wet clothes while leeches waited for us on every plant. I did not know how we had survived this long. I did not know if any of us would be here tomorrow.

16 Rocks Don't Fly

For two and a half years, I kept working, with not enough to eat and not enough sleep. The Khmer Rouge were always there with their guns pointed, yelling at us to work faster. One night I got off work and lay down to sleep at about ten o'clock. Then I heard a noise close by that I never heard before. I thought, *Maybe there's a wild animal in the jungle.* Elephants, bears, tigers, and snakes all came out at night to find food. I could hear something but couldn't see in the dark. I tapped my friend and whispered, "Did you hear that sound?"

He said, "Maybe it's the Khmer Rouge."

"Why would they come out at night like this? Maybe it's just animals."

My friend agreed that it was animals. I tried to go to sleep. The noise lasted a half hour longer, and then it was quiet.

We looked all around where the noise was, but we saw nothing damaged or broken. My friend was scared and said, "Maybe it was ghosts."

"It might have been ghosts," I answered, "but don't be afraid of ghosts." We had been living with ghosts by pulling dead bodies from the water for two years.

When we worked that day, and I was still thinking of the noise in the night, my friend said, "Bun, don't think about all that. Just keep working, and don't break any equipment."

I said, "You are right," but in my mind, I tried to figure out why animals would be close to us at night.

That night, we went back to where we had slept the previous night. Same spot. I talked quietly to my friend and asked how he was doing with the work.

"Tired," he said.

"Me too," I told him.

He asked, "Is there any way I can find a snake to eat, like I did before?"

I said, "The Khmer Rouge will kill us if we look. They killed two people who ate an unclean snake. Keep your eyes open for anything to eat that comes, so we can gain some energy back."

"I try all the time to do what you've told me," he said, "but my stomach is still empty."

We tried to sleep and think about tomorrow and the one cup of rice soup and chunk of salt we would eat after we worked. I closed my eyes and saw my parents, my brothers, and my sister in our house. I thought of the vehicles, bicycles, and people walking, talking, and laughing. I remembered the New Year's celebrations we had, with good food, relatives, and the games we played. I thought of the fun we had back then.

Then I looked at my sleeping friends. We were sleeping on hammocks made of old clothing, tied to the trees. My crew had been given these late that year. I told myself I needed to sleep too. I tried to sleep, but then I heard a noise—the same sound as last night but close to my bed. I saw rocks roll near my bed. I woke up my friend and said, "Listen! Do you hear that noise?"

"Yes. Maybe the Khmer Rouge are coming to take the crew."

"It couldn't be the Khmer Rouge," I said, "because they would not come out on a night like this. It might be ghosts, because the dead were very hungry when they died. Maybe they just want food." I then joked that I wanted to talk to the ghosts, because they would know where the food was around here. They could fly, swim, and go anywhere to see food, but we were stuck here on the ground. My friend laughed at me.

I felt something hit my leg. At first, I didn't know what it was, but later, I discovered it was a rock.

Then it was quiet. I stayed awake until about eleven o'clock, but no more rocks came, so I went to sleep.

When I woke up, I saw a rock. I thought, *Rocks don't fly. How did it get here?*

I told the Khmer Rouge that I had to go to relieve myself, but instead, I walked straight to where the noise was. I saw one spot where the plants were smashed down, as if someone had sat there. I ran back to my crew and told them what I'd found, saying, "I don't think it was ghosts or animals!"

My friend told the Khmer Rouge that he had to go to relieve himself. When he came back, we were all called to get up and go to work. While we worked, my friend whispered to me that he had seen the spot too.

We worked close together, watching the Khmer Rouge.

I said, "Something's not right." I told him at the end of the day that I would stay awake and watch to see if the rocks came again.

PART TWO

The Cambodian Freedom Army

17 *The Escape*

That night in August 1978, I lay wide awake. At exactly the same time, more rocks came from the nearby jungle. I woke my friend quickly and told him to watch with me. I wanted to see who it was. I grabbed a rock from the ground and threw it back. Then the rock came flying back to me. Whoa!

My heart was beating very hard. I told my friend, "Something is out there. You go check it out; I'll stay here."

He said, "No, Bun, you go! You are not scared."

I decided to throw one more rock. After I threw it, I saw a flashlight blinking. "I saw a light out there!" I said. "The Khmer Rouge never hide like that. They never play a game like this. If they wanted to kill us, they would just come and get us."

My friend was shaking with fear. "Bun, don't go!"

I said, "I need to see what is out there. You stay here."

I told him that if I went out there and came back, I would be alive. If I didn't come back, that would mean the Khmer Rouge had taken me away, and I was dead.

"Be careful," he said.

I stood up and looked around. The Khmer Rouge were in their houses, laughing and playing.

I thought, *It's ten at night. They can't see me. I don't need to ask them for permission to relieve myself.*

I took many deep breaths, and then I went slowly toward the jungle, taking a stick with me that I used to carry buckets.

As I got closer, I said quietly, "Who are you?"

The flashlight blinked on a shirt. As I got a little closer, someone said, "Come here. Come here."

I was trembling with fear. "Who are you?"

A voice said softly, "Come closer."

I got closer—but still not too close—and I said, "Are you Khmer Rouge?"

The voice said, "No, Cambodian Freedom Army."

I saw the light flash on clothing. The uniforms were not bright green but camouflage. When I saw that, I felt better. If their uniforms had been green, I'd be dead.

I walked a bit closer but looked back toward my friend. I was still very scared but decided to go even closer to the light. Finally, I saw the Cambodian Freedom Soldiers lying flat to the ground. There were two of them.

One said, "We have come here to help people who are hungry."

I asked, "Where do you live?"

"In the jungle."

"How many people do you have out there?" I asked.

"You don't want to know," one said. "We have come to help people. Go tell all of your friends that people are here to help. Tomorrow night, we will come here again. Come to see us. You go back to sleep now. Don't worry anymore. Come to this same place at the same hour."

"Okay," I said and left very fast. I had come out slowly, but now I was lighter, and I flew back. When I got back, three of my friends were awake, waiting for me. They asked, "Are you okay?"

"Yes, I'm fine! Don't worry anymore!" I told them. "I saw good people out there! We will go to sleep now and tomorrow night, you and I will go see them."

That night, I got no sleep at all. My heart was so excited that it was racing. Thoughts sped through my mind. *I am born again. My friends and I can be free again.* For so long, I had wondered how I could get away. I could not believe that there was someone here to help us. I told myself, *I have to go to them, no matter how hard it is. This is my day! Soon it will be better!*

The next morning, we went to work. I told my friends, one by one, that maybe we were lucky. One friend said, "Yes, I'm lucky. I get one scoop of rice soup a day."

I said, "Wait and see. I feel better now."

He said, "You're lucky? Maybe they will bring you to pull out dead bodies again."

That day, I told about fifty people about the soldiers. After work, we went back to our beds. Three friends sat with me to wait until ten o'clock.

I said, "Wait and listen. The Cambodian Freedom Soldiers will blink the lights again."

We looked out for the Khmer Rouge but did not see them. We moved flat on the ground to where the soldiers were. One of my friends saw the soldiers with his own eyes. He was so happy that he jumped over the two of us. I told him to be quiet, or the Khmer Rouge would hear him.

The two Cambodian Freedom Soldiers said, "Don't worry; from now on we will come help you."

I told my new friend, "It's good that you know someone will help us, but we'd better get back before the Khmer Rouge checks on us."

The soldiers told us that tomorrow, they would come to us for the last time. Tomorrow, we would find a safe place.

"Tomorrow morning, go to work, and tell everyone to be ready to move from this place," one soldier said. "Don't make a mistake by acting too excited or happy. Just be quiet and act like you always do."

At work, my friends and I told all two hundred of our crew. We all were happy. I saw a bit of a smile on my friend's face for the first time. We hoped that someday soon, we would eat good food. That night, the four of us went straight to the Cambodian Freedom Soldiers. One of them told us, "Tomorrow night, we will leave this place at ten at night."

"We have two hundred people," I said. "You have only two people and two guns. How can you help us?"

"Don't worry; be happy," he said.

"How can you cover two hundred people?" I asked again.

"We'll figure that out," the soldier said. "How many houses are there with Khmer Rouge inside?"

"Fifteen."

"We need fifteen people."

"Why?"

He only said, "We need them."

"I will find fifteen people."

He gave me a box of matches for fifteen people, one match for each house. Bamboo houses catch fire easily. He said, "Have them sit up at this same hour tomorrow. Tell them to be ready to get out and not to bring anything."

"We have nothing but our hammocks anyway," I told him.

They then gave me fifty flashlights to give to my crew. They showed me the technique to use when flashing the lights so the Khmer Rouge would not see us. "Tell the fifteen that after they start the houses on fire, they should look up in the sky to the chicken baby stars [a constellation] and go across the shape of the chicken to the west. Go in one line toward the stars."

One Cambodian Freedom Soldier would lead the front of the line and one would be last in line, to make sure that the houses burned and the fifteen got out.

That next night, we set the houses on fire at exactly 10:00 p.m.— the soldiers had given us a watch. The whole crew got out of there really fast. The Khmer Rouge ran out of their houses screaming, "Fire! Fire!"

They did not know that we had set the fires. We were heading away from the fires into the jungle as fast as we could go. A half hour later, we heard big and small cannons bombing every corner. The Khmer Rouge knew we had escaped.

At about ten thirty, the bombs began to land all around us. One hit the middle of our line. I could hear people screaming. The Khmer Rouge could hear the screaming too and aimed their cannons toward the sound.

We split up and broke the line. Everyone went a different way. Some did not know what to do and just hid behind trees. I could not tell which way to go, so I looked up at the chicken baby stars. Only five people were left with me out of two hundred. We kept walking through the thick jungle in the dark. We could not see our hands in front of our faces. We waved our hands in front of us until they bumped into a tree or bush. After two hours of slow progress, we stopped to take a break. I did not see anybody. We stayed there, without sleeping, until morning, trying to find our friends.

At around 1:10 a.m., two Cambodian Freedom Soldiers found us and told us to go straight ahead to where the Freedom Camp was. In our white clothes, we could not hide very well. At about 1:15 a.m., I told my friends to watch for our crew. We saw one person. I said to my friends, "Let's go to him."

I asked him where the others were, but he did not know. Maybe they were dead; the bomb had hit right behind him. He also did not know where the Cambodian Freedom Soldiers were.

The next morning, we found members of my work crew. Thirty-two of us now walked together in the jungle. We could not go into the open field where we would be seen. At about eight in the morning, we saw about ten people with one Freedom Soldier with them. He did not know where the other soldier was.

At about noon, the Cambodian Freedom Soldier told us to take a break, because it was safe there. The Cambodian Freedom Soldiers had food hidden in the jungle for us, so he said for us to wait while he got the food.

Five people went with him to carry the food. They brought back rice, fruit, and meat, which they cooked.

Everybody stood around the food, so hungry that they were shaking while it cooked. The smell of the food cooking almost drove us crazy, but at the same time, we knew that we had to be careful and not eat too much the first time. We had not had a full meal in so long a time that too much too fast might make us sick. The soldier told us that after we ate, we would go back and look for more of our crew.

When the food was ready to eat, he said, "Go ahead and help yourself."

My friend had eaten little food for two and a half years. He ate until he overloaded and got very sick.

I remembered that when I was in school, one of my teachers taught us how to eat safely if we ever went without food for a long time. He said, "If you have had no food for a long time, eat small amounts very slowly. Your stomach is not ready for food."

The friend who ate too much sat down. He could not breathe. Within two hours, he passed away. Everybody just stood and looked at him. Someone said, "We are sorry that you have been away from those criminals for just one day, and now you are dead."

We prayed for him. He had gotten half a night of freedom. We buried him right there. I thought, *That was far more than the people in the field got when they died.*

Then we walked away from him.

18 | *The Freedom Camp*

Three days passed. We spent each day trying to find the rest of our people, but we did not find them. The Cambodian Freedom Soldier said, "Let's go to a safe place."

We walked for three more days. When I asked him how far we had to go, he said it would be only one half day more. I looked back; everybody was very tired. He said, "Five more kilometers, and you will see freedom."

Everyone was so happy that they sang all the way. The Cambodian Freedom Soldier said, "Go ahead and make all the noise you want. There are no Khmer Rouge here." A half hour later, after walking up a large hill, we heard a noise and saw the Cambodian Freedom Camp! All our people rushed forward, running and telling each other, "Come on! Hurry up! We see the Cambodian Freedom people!"

The whole camp came forward to welcome us. It was the first time they had seen people who were starving like we were. We had been gone for two and a half years in the fields. We were the first to come out.

Young and old, boys and girls, the people cried when they saw us. They asked if we had we seen their brother, sister, father, mother, uncle—people went in every direction, looking at us to see if they would find their relatives. We were all boys, no girls or families, because only boys worked the fields. Then the people called a few of us to follow them. They cooked for us and gave us clothes. We took off our filthy white clothes and put on clean colored clothes.

One family took five of us; others went to other houses. I had a lot of scratches and cuts from running in the jungle. They gave us good food and warm blankets. If we needed anything, they helped us right away.

When I saw these people helping, I thought of my parents, brothers, and sister. As I ate, I choked up, thinking about them. Some people asked me about my family, and I told them we had been split up. "You are my family now," I said. That was all I had. We all called these people Dad and Mom. I cried, but there were still no tears.

The meals seemed like feasts. They had meat and chicken from Thailand, vegetables from their garden, and fruit. It was so good. Mealtimes were happy times—good food, good company.

The five of us stayed with our new family for three days. We were on borderland between Cambodia and Thailand, where the Khmer Rouge could not get us. Then the soldiers of the camp called us to a meeting. We went down to wait for the man in charge of the Cambodian Freedom Army. We called him the Big Boss.

At this time, we saw another group, about seventy-five people, and the soldier who had helped us escape was with them. These were the people we had been looking for in the jungle, but they had gotten here before us!

The Big Boss came to ask us how we were doing. He called me "kid." I told him that during the three nights when the Freedom Soldiers had hidden in the dark and threw rocks at us, I was scared to death. But we were lucky, because we had made it away from the Khmer Rouge.

He said, "You have a new home here. You are safe; you can go where you want and do what you want."

He asked the escapees about the families who helped us and then told the Cambodian Freedom Soldiers to find a place for us to stay, away from the families. The soldiers gave us supplies, so we could cook for ourselves and take care of ourselves. We had a house with a roof, and we were dry and warm. The people would bring us food that they had cooked at their homes. They did not want to leave us; they wanted to stay and take care of us until our muscles came back. We were skin and bones with sunken eyes and our hair had fallen out. We stayed there for three weeks. The Big Boss came and checked on us every week.

I thought of my family and our life as it had been. Memories of family life came to me—what my mother had said about the importance of family; how I had worked with my sister in the restaurant.

After one month, someone told us that we needed exercise for our bodies. We went to the water and swam for an hour, chasing each other around and playing, and then went back to our house. After we had one month of good food and rest, our skin became red again, not white like it had been.

The families came to take us out into a big field, where they joined us in playing games, dancing, and singing. The kids chased us around in fun. Then I sat down next to the old people and asked, "Why do people do things like the Khmer Rouge did? Why do they make people work to death like that?"

One old man said, "When you grow older, you cannot worry about it. That is why we came to be with you and have fun."

We went back to our camp at eleven at night. I had never learned to dance, because I had spent my teenage years in the Killing Fields. That year, however, I learned to dance and sing. I tried to have fun and forget about my experiences. I had eaten flies from my face, and I had prayed at every corner.

At night, I would think about when I was young and my mother was good to people and gave them food when they needed it. Maybe this is what saved me.

Two months passed quickly. The Big Boss came to see how we were doing. I said, "I am strong. I am ready to go down and help people."

The Boss joked with me. "You can't hold up your own body. You have only been here two months."

A month later, a second boss came to see us. We told him we were fine—good food and drinks had made us strong. We were ready to help people. He said they would take us for some experience in the jungle. The sessions would be from five in the morning to noon. My friend Hood said, "What? Five in the morning? I'm still asleep."

At five o'clock, whistles blew. The crew was still asleep. One of the soldiers called to us, "Wake up, wake up! Only a half hour left! Line up in that field. When you hear the whistles, follow the Cambodian Freedom leader."

They gave us too much physical training that first day—push-ups, running, swimming for four hours at a time. We were all tired. None of us had experience as soldiers. At noon, we stopped training to eat. We met for training each day from five in the morning until noon and then ate, and then the whistle would blow, calling us back to our training. We swam after lunch for one hour straight. For one month, we trained in Cambodian, Thai, and French techniques. We learned about walking and surviving in the jungle and how to use weapons. We walked single file in the jungle, and we learned to be watchful. The enemy might be hiding anywhere.

At the end of the month, the leader said, "You all did well. You learned good techniques. In six months, you will go down to help people get out."

Every day, seven days a week, we trained. The second and third bosses watched us to see which of us was smarter, faster, and good at using the techniques we had learned

They would shout, "Go under the barbed wire. Keep your heads down. Be careful where you go. There is poop there. Go into the water. Duck your heads underwater for two minutes." Another day, we ducked our heads for three minutes and then five minutes—that was the maximum.

After two and a half months of training, the second boss said that some of us kids were very smart and did not need to train for the whole six months. Some of us were ready to go now.

We went back to camp and talked among ourselves, wondering which of us was ready. We all wanted to stop training. It was hard. We had to crawl on the ground—and there was human waste on the ground—while real bullets were shot above us.

I thought, *I need to go. I have those people in my mind's eye. I know how to help them escape.*

My energy was back now. Exercise had made me stronger than when I was resting.

The next day, the Big Boss brought a list of names of those who were ready to stop training and could take care of themselves. Out of 107 of us, ten names were on the list. I was number two on the list! I would be going to Cambodia to rescue people.

We trained for another week and then had tests for a week. The ten of us were taken away from the others. We slept together, ate together, and became great friends.

They took all 107 of us to a warehouse. Inside was a map on a big screen. They asked if I had gone to school in Cambodia and if I was I good at math. They tested all of us. I passed right away. They showed us the map of where the Khmer Rouge were located. The Freedom Army was located on the border between Cambodia and Thailand. The Khmer Rouge controlled most of the country and all the cities.

The second day, they pulled out cannons, bombs, and mines to show us the different kinds and what they were used for. Some, like the B-69, were used to blow up trucks, tanks, and buildings. Others, like the smaller B-60, were used for blowing up people. We got three days' worth of training in one day. They trained us in the shapes, sizes, and origins of mines. There was a special mine from China that we needed to look for if we were crossing water. We learned how to place mines and how to spot and remove them in the jungle. We learned to look for traps made of bamboo and to look for the 69 mine.

The 69 mine was about the size of a quart bottle. It had three prongs on the top. It was designed to be placed in the ground with a leaf on top of it. As soon as someone stepped on the mine, the bomb would shoot up five feet in the air and explode in a thirty-five-foot circle.

We were shown tank mines that required many pounds of pressure to set off. We were taught how to disarm them. Later, we would play with these big mines, using them like balls and toys after taking out the fuse.

After a week, we were taken into the jungle for a test. The Freedom Army, the leaders of which were Prom Vet and San Sand, had set up mines everywhere in the jungle. We were all sent out in different directions. Could we find our way through the jungle and over hills, with bombs and mines everywhere? To pass the test, we had to find three mines. We had one week to do so. Soldiers walked behind us to see how we did. The bombs and mines had no explosives inside. They were fake, so none of us would get hurt.

It did not take long for me to find the first two mines. One was on a tree—I'd seen a broken limb on the tree. Then I saw three needles poking out of the leaves on the ground—this was a 69 mine. I removed it, leaf by leaf, and then took it out. I found the third on a hill. I saw the needle sticking out from the ground. It was the kind that had an invisible string. The soldiers high-fived me and said, "Bun, you are really smart! You are finished—you got three! You can go back to camp."

I was the first one back. Seven guys never found any mines. After I passed the test, a soldier took me to see the Big Boss. He said, "Congratulations. You are a smart kid. You can go help people now."

I had more extensive training that day. I was taught how to use each gun and shown which weapon was best for different types of fighting.

In jungle warfare, our Big Boss, Prom Vet, said, "I prefer the heavier AK-47 over the lighter M-16, and this is why: we have tested these guns in the jungle. We soaked the Chinese AK-47s in dirty water and took them out. They fired perfectly. No problem. We then we got the US M-16s wet, and the barrel split apart when we fired it. Then we stuck the guns in mud and got them very dirty. The AK-47 fired sixty bullets. The M-16 jammed. Then we shot the guns at rows of banana trees. The bullets of the M-16s would go into three and stop. The AK-47s would go through four trees and come out the other side.

"In live fighting, the AK-47 will shoot through two soldiers easily. The M-16 bullet will stop in one soldier. If we fire fifteen rounds through an M-16, the barrel will get very hot and could split apart. The AK-47 can shoot thirty-sixty rounds with no problems. In conclusion, in jungle warfare, the AK-47 is a superior weapon. It has better range and won't jam. This is very important in fighting the Khmer Rouge in the jungles."

We were taught how to disassemble the AK-47 while blindfolded. It got to the point where I could put the gun together faster with my eyes closed.

We played games like this, tearing the guns apart and putting them back together quickly. The slow soldiers had to get down on all fours and carry the fast soldiers on their backs around a circle. This made everyone laugh.

We were told that each crew of ten soldiers would be given one 60- and one 80-millimeter cannon in case they ran into tanks or found Khmer Rouge hidden in buildings.

We would also be given a machine gun that could fire one hundred rounds in ten seconds. This gun was more powerful than the AK-47. It was also very heavy. It had three legs, which unfolded when set on the ground. Later, I would learn to like this gun.

We were taught how to be very accurate with the B-69 and B-60 cannons. These shoulder cannons shot shells a long way. With careful training, we learned to pick out targets and take them out with great accuracy. Six shells were all a soldier could carry with this weapon. They were very heavy. When we fired one of these cannons, fire blew out the side, and the shell lit up the sky.

The terrain of western Cambodia. The Freedom Camp was on the side of a mountain like this one, a three-hour walk from the Thailand border.

19 My First Freedom Mission

It was March 1979, a hot time of year. After my weeks of training, I was excited to go on my first mission. I took a break for one week, and went back to be with the other trainees.

During the day, when seven were still testing, three of us played with the other members of our unit. One of them said, "When you go, we have food for you to take with you."

The next morning, I talked with the Big Boss and asked him when I would be going to Cambodia. He said, "Take one more week off."

After another week of rest, good food, and good sleep, I was ready to go. There were three people in my crew and four Cambodian Freedom Soldiers.

The people from camp brought food for us. That day, seven of us walked away from camp. After all the training, I was sure the soldiers would give me a gun. But they gave me heavy sacks of food instead. My weapon was a stick with a knife taped to the end. Only the soldiers had guns.

I carried a large backpack loaded with a sixty-pound bag of rice, cans of food, meat, candy, a flashlight, Band-Aids, and extra clothes. My pack weighed more than one hundred pounds; I weighed about eighty-nine pounds at that time and was five foot three. We followed the soldiers, walking slowly for a mile and then taking a break. My back hurt. There was no way to walk for longer than that without a break.

We entered the jungle the next day. The terrain was difficult, the walking slow. To get energy, I thought of the Khmer Rouge and the starving people. I got mad. I wanted to save the people. This helped me to walk with the heavy load.

I asked the soldiers how long it would be before we got there. They said, "Four days, with these heavy loads of food. Coming back, it will be lighter. We are taking all this food for the people out there."

We saw many monkeys and birds in the jungle. The leaves and ground were covered with leeches. When we took breaks, I often felt something itchy around my toes. I took my boots off and found leeches between my toes, filling up with blood. The soldiers gave me and the others salt in a piece of cloth. We were told to wipe it on our legs to keep the leeches away. The soldiers gave me Band-Aids to stop the bleeding when I pulled the leeches off.

This was the first day I had ever walked a long distance with heavy boots on my feet. I was not used to having shoes. We walked and stopped, walked and stopped, for two days. Then we found a place to hide the food. The soldiers said we were still two days from the city, but it would take only one day when we came back with the people. We would be going light and fast. We left seven backpacks of food right there.

We walked for two more days. We saw a huge, black-and-yellow python, as big around as a five-gallon bucket, and followed the snake's path so we didn't have to make a new path. We prayed for the snake and that it would not be killed. Snakes were considered the kings and queens of the Cambodian jungle. We asked for the snake's help when we went down to help the people.

Soon it was night. We rested there, far away from the snake. One more day, and we would be in the city. We piled our extra food there under a tent and left two soldiers there to guard the food.

We went on with dried fish, rice, and water for one day. We carried extra food for people we might encounter who were hungry. As we walked toward the city, the soldiers talked to us about techniques, how to get into the village, and how to approach the people who were trapped there by the Khmer Rouge. One soldier stayed behind to signal. One soldier and my group went in three directions. In an hour, we all returned to share how many people we had seen and who we had met. We had seen about fifteen hundred adult people in the village that we would try to take out.

For three nights, we planned our strategy. The Freedom Army soldiers told us that even though we were here to help the people, they would be scared of us. The Khmer Rouge had made them fear everything. We were told that we would have to trick the people into coming with us. This was my first time to help, and I worried a lot because there were so many people.

That day, I took off my uniform and dressed in white, like the people in the village. Then I went into the village. I met an old man and woman, walking together. They were very thin, and their eyes were dark and sunken. Their clothes were dirty and ragged. They spoke in very low voices, so that I had to listen closely to hear what they said.

I asked the man, "Uncle, where are you going?"

"I am going to get something to eat," he answered.

"Where are your kids?"

"The Khmer Rouge took them away."

"What kind of food do you eat?"

"Whatever we can find. We have not eaten for two days."

"Where are the people of the village?"

"They are in the jungle, looking for food. Where have you come from?"

"The other side of the village."

He saw that my body and skin looked different. He said, "Your village is better than ours. You have meat on your bones."

I said, "We work hard and have a little food left over. The Khmer Rouge make food for us."

I had to tell him this so he would come with us. If I told him we were Cambodian Freedom Fighters, he would not believe me. I was dressed like him, in white. I had no evidence that I was a soldier here to rescue him. No one in the village knew about a Cambodian Freedom Army.

He said, "Maybe we will go that way."

I said, "Yes, I can tell you where to get good food. How far is your house?"

"Ten kilometers away."

I asked to look in his backpack and saw that he had a one-foot round potato. "You have only one potato?"

"Yes."

"Can you sit down and talk with us?" I asked the old man. We sat down together, and I asked him, "Where do you work right now?"

"We work on-call. Sometimes the Khmer Rouge have us work, and sometimes we don't work. On our days off, we look for food."

"How many people are in your village?" I asked.

"Not many, maybe a thousand. This village is no good. There is no food, so people move away. Five or ten families just went to find another place."

"What about the Khmer Rouge?" I asked. "Do they take care of you?"

"Sometimes they come; sometimes not at all."

"How are you doing?" I asked him again.

"Sometimes we are lucky and find fruit; sometimes we go to bed hungry."

"Do you like to eat good food?"

He put up his two hands to pray and said, "It doesn't matter how hard we have to work, if we get some food."

"Can you do me a favor?" I asked.

He said, "What can I do for you?"

"Can you follow me? I can find you something to eat; just follow me."

I could hear the fear in his voice as he asked, "Are you sure?"

"I look like your kid, and you look like my father," I reassured him. "I am seventeen. I will not hurt you."

"My kids are eighteen, seventeen, and sixteen," he said. "One boy and two girls."

"When did they walk away from you?"

"In1975, when the Khmer Rouge took over the city. From that day, I haven't seen them."

I asked, "Can you give their names to me? Maybe I'll find them in my village." Then I picked up a flat rock and handed it to the old man. He wrote the names on the rock, and I put it in my pocket. I told him that I would let him know if I found his children.

"Where are your parents?" he asked me.

"They live with me," I answered. "They eat good food and have lots of stuff. You could go to my village. You know me now." Then I asked him, "How can you walk far away from your home? Won't the Khmer Rouge find you?"

He shook his head. "No, the Khmer Rouge already know we have no food, and we have to look in the jungle."

"Do you want to come to my city for food? It's one day's walk."

He turned to his wife and said, "Can we go with this kid?"

"That kid would not lie," his wife said. "If he says they have food, then they have food. We have not had food for how many days?"

I told them, "Maybe it's time you come to see my city. You can tell other people to get food from my city too." Then I said, "Mom and Dad, are you ready? Let's go."

The old man nodded and said, "Yes."

Together, we walked to the jungle.

I told one of my crew to walk ahead to get a little bit of food and meet us halfway. The old couple and I walked and talked quietly until we came upon one of my crew coming back to us with food. He had changed out of the white clothes of the workers and into his Freedom Army uniform.

When the old couple saw him, they asked nervously, "Who is he?"

I said, "Don't panic. He is part of my crew."

Their eyes opened wide. "How do you do this?" the man asked.

Instead of answering, I led them to the soldier with the food. He opened his pack and took out some rice and meat for the couple to eat.

The wife said that she couldn't believe she had found good people. My soldier and I cried together when she said that.

The man said, "I like you, kid."

When he said "kid," my heart jumped. I thought of my mom's voice, and I cried again.

I told him, "I like you too."

Then the man prayed for us. We shared our stories. I asked them if they knew of my parents, but they did not.

The day was still early, and I wanted to go back in the city to find more people, but we talked a little longer. The man asked me where I came from and what my parents did.

I told him how the Khmer Rouge questioned me and gave me white clothes and took me away from my family. I said that I had worked twenty-three hours a day without enough food or sleep and that my hair fell out. I said, "Mom and Dad, you are lucky. You can walk on your own and find food. I could not go anywhere. The Khmer Rouge watched every minute. I ate one scoop of rice soup and salt a day until the Cambodian Freedom Soldiers found me." I explained that I also had been worried about who the Freedom Soldiers were when I first saw them, but they had brought us food and my crew had escaped that night with them. I described how we were bombed one hour later by the Khmer Rouge's cannons but that a soldier took us away to a safe place. "My body was just skin and bones when I reached the Freedom Camp," I explained, "but now, after just three months of rest, I have come back to help find people. I know they have no food, and I remember the hunger and how I ate anything that came close to my face."

The man said, "It's time to do something, because the Khmer Rouge don't care about any of us young or old people. They use us all like slaves."

"Can you do me a favor?" I asked him.

"Yes, whatever you need. I have a little energy after eating."

"How many people are in the city?"

He shrugged, unsure of the answer. "People go in and out. The city is very quiet."

"Tomorrow, we will go in and look for people," I instructed. "We will talk to them. You tell them that we will find a better place with good food. Tell people to tell others."

"Kid, this kind of food is hard to find," he told me. "When I tell them, they will come in a second."

The next morning, we went back to the city. I said, "Tell everybody not to make a mistake. Do not tell the people we are Cambodian Freedom Soldiers."

He said, "Kid, I am old enough to be careful when I talk to them."

I told him to meet me at exactly noon in this spot.

When he came back, he said, "When the people saw me, they knew something was up. One night with food made a difference in my appearance. Some of the people want to get out. They have no food, and I told them I had found some."

"We have to get everyone out of here quickly," I told him. "Don't wait. I will give you about four or five hours. Around nine or ten tonight, we will get out."

He said there were about a thousand people. I made it clear that we had to get everyone out. The Khmer Rouge would kill anyone left behind.

"Go back and tell them to set up for tonight," I instructed him.

He said, "Don't worry; we have plenty of time."

At about nine that night, we set up twelve mines outside the far end of the city, where the Khmer Rouge were. The first explosion went off at ten o'clock. The Khmer Rouge looked in that direction, not toward the part of city where all the people were getting out. After that first one, bombs went off every ten seconds.

My soldiers and I went in and took the people back to our camp. The young people, both men and women, would join the Freedom

Army. There were sixty to seventy babies, and I thought about my baby brother, that a hungry baby cried, and that the Khmer Rouge would hear that. I told the people that I had special food to give the babies. When they cried, we would put this food in their mouths.

The soldiers were in front, but one was at the back with three of us, to make sure the Khmer Rouge did not follow.

We left a couple of mines behind us on the road. The people moved very fast. I had no gun to protect myself and was scared to death. We walked through the jungle until midnight and then took a break. The people were scared to stop, but we told them it was safe, even though we were scared too—we stopped because we did not know where our soldiers were. Somehow, we had become separated. We had no guns to protect ourselves from the Khmer Rouge, so after a short rest, we took off.

We kept walking through the night. At about one in the morning, we stopped to talk. Some people were very scared because they had never been deep in the jungle before. Many asked how far we needed to go.

I answered, "Not far now. Only two more days."

The people wanted to keep walking without stopping, but I told them that we needed to take a rest—a half-hour break. They were still very scared. They did not know where we were taking them.

I joked with them. "What can you do now? Can you find your way back home now? And why? What's there?" Then I said seriously, "I was with the Khmer Rouge for two and a half years. I know how terrible it is."

When the sun came up, we continued onward. At about ten o'clock, we stopped and ate a little bit of the food in the backpacks. I told the people that this was a safe place. "The Khmer Rouge know that if they come this far into the jungle, it will be very dangerous for them," I explained.

"Are you sure it is safe here?" a man asked quietly.

I said, "Just look at the equipment and the food."

"Where did the food come from?" he asked.

"Thailand," I answered.

"I have never seen the Thailand border."

"You will," I assured him.

The next morning as we walked, we opened two more backpacks of food. The people's expressions had lightened up considerably. They talked and sang as they walked; they laughed and joked. We kept walking toward the safety of our camp. We walked in the jungle, because if we walked in the open field, the white clothes would be seen more easily.

When we got to the place where we had hidden the food, and the people saw the uniforms of the Cambodian Freedom Army soldiers, they all cheered. I heard one person say, "I didn't know if any Cambodian Freedom Soldiers were still alive." We took the food out, and the people cheered again.

After we ate, we continued walking for the rest of the day, until we reached our camp. The people who had escaped with me the first time came to welcome the new ones. One of them said, "You will have a new life from now on, with good food and good people."

Then I went back to my camp of ten friends to see how they were doing. "Did you pass the mine tests?" I asked.

One of them said, "No, Bun, it is not easy to find the mines."

"Keep going," I instructed all of them. "If you can't pass the test and you step on a 69 mine, you will be dead."

They wanted to know about the mission from which I'd just returned, so I told them about finding the people in the city and that I had been scared when we took all the people out. "All I had was a stick and a knife to protect us from the Khmer Rouge," I told them. "But I had good luck this first time. We got a lot of people out, and only a few were hurt from stepping on mines. The Khmer Rouge did not find us with their bombs. Everything went smoothly, and I am very thankful that I did not get hurt."

After I talked with my friends, I went over to see all the people from the city. They were talking together, telling their stories to my people, and crying. Too many stories. I walked around these families and asked them if they knew of my mom or my dad. They did not.

I told them, "From now on, don't worry; be happy. You got away from the criminals."

I asked my friends—those who had escaped with me the first time—to take good care of these new people. Then I went to my tent and thought about my parents.

I remembered the times when we visited relatives in Thailand. I remembered how we all worked together in the restaurant. If they were still alive, I would find them.

20 Bun Gets His Gun

The next morning, I woke up at five o'clock. The number-two boss called me, my crew of seven, and two Cambodian Freedom Soldiers into a meeting. He thanked all the crew very much for saving people's lives. Now there would be good food, good sleep, and no more hunger for these people.

I told him, "Four months have passed since I escaped. I trained very hard and passed all the tests. You sent me down to help, but I had no gun; only two soldiers had guns. When we took the people out, my heart was beating very fast. I asked myself how we could do this with too many people and not enough guns."

Then the two Cambodian Freedom Soldiers talked to the Big Boss. "Bun went into the city the first night and found the people," one said. "The second night, he went back again and got more people. Bun did all the work to get the people out."

The Big Boss thanked me, and I said, "You are welcome. It was a first time for me."

Then he said, "Everyone stay strong. Take a break."

I went to see my old friends, the 107. They were still training. They asked how it went, going down to Cambodia.

"It was fun," I answered. "You all had better train hard so you can help rescue people."

Then I went to visit with the old people we had rescued, and I enjoyed some time with them.

Two days passed. The Big Boss called me to another meeting.

"I heard about your efforts when you went down to Cambodia," he said to me. Then he motioned to some soldiers and said, "Bring the case out."

I didn't know what was inside. Boss number two opened the case. I saw a brand new AK-47. I was happy and excited when I saw it. Now I could protect myself and the people I rescued from the Khmer Rouge.

They gave AK-47s to me and my three friends. The Big Boss said, "This gun is your life. Take it everywhere. Sleep with it. Don't let it leave your hands."

We were very excited, and I said to my friend, "We have had a week's break. Let's go get more people out of Cambodia."

"Yes," he agreed, "we had only our bare hands and were scared to death. Now we have guns. Let's go again."

I went to check on all the new people to see how they were doing. They came up to me and thanked me for saving their lives. They asked me what they could do for me, and I said, "The Cambodian Freedom Soldiers saved me, so now I want to help other people. I'm going into Cambodia again. We have my crew plus six soldiers, so that makes ten. You could set up enough food for us to take for the week."

The next morning, all the people we had rescued watched us go, and they prayed for us.

On our second night out, we took a break just before dark. I told two of my crew to walk one mile around us to check it out. When they returned, they reported that they had seen about fifteen Khmer Rouge sitting down to cook dinner. More of us went to take a look. We saw about fifty of them. They were yelling and talking loudly.

Some of our soldiers reported. "More Khmer Rouge are behind us, so we need to find another route out of here."

There were only ten of us soldiers, and the Khmer Rouge had over fifty.

"Maybe they knew we were here and that we were coming to rescue people," someone suggested.

We sat quietly, thinking how to get out.

Suddenly, we saw two Khmer Rouge coming our way, straight toward us. We decided to grab them, quickly and quietly.

We grabbed them without making a sound, and they dropped their guns and put their hands up. The other Khmer Rouge were about a mile away. The two we caught might have been lost. After we tied them up, we asked how many were with them and why they were around here. They said they were on a patrol to find the people who had escaped. They were afraid and had peed their pants. One soldier, who told me his name was Meng, cried, "Please don't kill me!"

"We will not kill you," I replied. "We are Cambodian Freedom Soldiers, and we do not kill people, except in self-defense."

One of my soldiers said, "Do not try to run away. If you do, I'll shoot you in the leg."

"How many of your men are out there?" I asked.

"A lot," Meng answered.

I told Meng and the other Khmer Rouge, "What my soldier said was true; if you try to run, we will shoot you in the leg."

When they said they wouldn't run anymore, we grabbed the two Khmer Rouge and put them at the back of our crew. We kept their AK-47s.

Two hours later, we heard the sound of guns. I asked the Khmer kids, "Who is fighting with whom?"

"This afternoon we saw some Cambodian Freedom Soldiers and fought with them," Meng said.

We could hear fighting not far from us. Five of us went to check. As we got closer, I could see the soldiers wearing the same uniform as we wore. We shot three times—that was a signal that I could see them. They fired three shots to signal that they would come find us.

When they reached us, one said, "There are a lot of Khmer Rouge out there, and it will take at least an hour to fight them."

"Where are you going?" I asked.

"To Cambodia, to get people out."

"It is a good thing we met you," I said, "We can help each other."

I told them to bring their crew this way. Combining our crews made twenty-five soldiers. Then we went back to where the other five from my crew were waiting for us. They said they had fought Khmer Rouge for an hour with nobody winning or losing. We got away from there quickly, so the Khmer Rouge could not fire on us. After fleeing through the jungle for an hour, we took a break.

The next morning, we sent two of our soldiers home with the two prisoners. The Big Boss had said to catch Khmer Rouge and send them back alive, so that we could show the Thai authorities we were fighting the Khmer Rouge. This way, the Thai government would send food to our camp.

From there, we went straight to the Cambodian village.

As our crew approached the village, we reminded each other that the Khmer Rouge might know where we were because we had fought with them yesterday.

We got to the edge of the jungle and split up into two groups. I was left with eight soldiers. We got near the village and could see Khmer Rouge everywhere in the nearby jungle. They were waiting for us.

I told my crew, "This is not good. We are not here to fight but to save people. We don't have enough guns or soldiers to take on the whole Khmer Rouge army."

My crew worked their way around the village, looking for a way in. The Khmer Rouge spotted us and opened fire. I told our crew to fight but to back up quickly. "Don't go forward."

We kept moving backward and shooting at the Khmer Rouge until their guns quieted. I told my crew, "Let's go home. We have had two fights with the Khmer Rouge already. We don't want to lose anyone or get hurt. We are not here to kill anyone."

21 The Blood Brothers

After we got back to the Freedom Camp, I went to see the Big Boss. I told him about our fights with the Khmer Rouge. He said that we had done the right thing in coming back. He was thankful no one was injured. He told us to take a break.

I went to talk with the new people, the ones we had rescued, and asked them how they were doing. "Don't worry," I told them. "The people will take care of you."

The next morning, the Big Boss gave me thirty more soldiers. I trained the soldiers, showing them how to escape, how to hide, and how to fight.

The two Khmer Rouge soldiers we had captured were put to work in the food warehouse. I thought this was very fitting that the Khmer Rouge, who had been in charge of starving people to death, were now in charge of feeding them.

Meng talked to me each day. He was about the same age as me and about the same size. I could tell that he liked me. He said, "I want to go with you back into Cambodia to help rescue people."

"I do not trust you," I answered. "The Khmer Rouge killed so many people. How can we trust any Khmer Rouge soldier? How do we know that you will not betray us or turn around and shoot us?"

Still, Meng was persistent. Every day that I was in camp, Meng would find me and ask again, "Can I become a Freedom Soldier?"

"No, just keep working to feed people."

One day when Meng found me, I asked him, "Why did you become a Khmer Rouge?"

"I had no choice," he answered. "They had captured my family and would have killed my parents if I did not become a soldier. After I joined them, they killed my family anyway. I am an orphan now."

Still, I refused to let him become a Freedom Soldier.

From that point on, my crew was very busy, making trips through the jungle to rescue more people. I kept thinking about all the people starving in the cities. I thought about my parents and my family. Each day in camp, I became more restless. I felt that I could not stay in camp for more than three days. I had to go back into Cambodia and save people and look for my parents.

I took a crew on rescue missions twice a month. From most villages, we were able to take out two or three hundred people at a time. We also found many people lost in the jungle and brought them back to the Freedom Camp.

Life went like this: two weeks on a mission, rest at home for three days, and then head back out for another mission.

On each mission, I would ask people in the village if they knew of my parents. They never did. Eventually, I gave up hope of ever finding them. Now, saving the people was my reason to keep going.

During my brief stays in camp, my soldiers and I played games together. One of our favorite games was to collect all our AK-47s, take them apart, and mix up the pieces. Then we would have a race to see who could get his gun back together the fastest. AK-47 parts are interchangeable. We could grab the parts from another gun and stick it on our own. This was fun. We always gave the winner a small prize. The soldier who was last or who could not put his gun back together had to do push-ups. To have more fun, we would sit on his back as he did the push-ups to make him work even harder.

One day, after we had returned from a mission with more people, Meng again asked me, "May I join your soldiers?"

That day, I sat down and talked with him. I asked him, "Have you killed people for the Khmer Rouge?"

"No, I never did. I would not shoot anyone. May I go into Cambodia with you on your next mission? I know where there is looted gold and jewelry left by the Khmer Rouge. I can help you find the gold and learn how to stay away from the Khmer Rouge."

I went to my boss and told him about Meng, the gold, and his request to join my crew.

The Big Boss was very suspicious of him. "He just spent years killing our people. How can we trust him?"

"Meng said he never killed anyone."

"All right, but be very careful."

I decided to take Meng with me on the next mission. He was guarded by my soldiers twenty-four hours a day. We would take no chances.

True to his word, Meng led us safely past the Khmer Rouge. On our way home with the people, Meng took us to large dumps of gold jewelry that were left at certain places in the jungle. My soldiers came home with watches, rings, and jewelry that they set on tables so the Big Boss could see what we had found. He was elated. He could sell the gold and jewelry in Thailand and buy food for the people in the camp.

After that, Meng was allowed to go on another expedition. Eventually, I told him that there was only one thing for the two of us to do: become brothers. This way, we could finally trust each other. In Cambodia we have a ritual where two friends cut themselves and pour their blood into a container. After the blood is mixed, they add wine and then drink it. From then on those two friends are brothers. When one gets married, the other also is married. If one has a fight, the other has a fight.

We went to see a wise old man who knew Cambodian customs. He would be our witness. Six of us soldiers went that day. Meng and I made the cuts and mixed the blood in a bowl. The old man added a little bit of wine. Each of us took a turn drinking from the bowl.

Meng and I were now blood brothers. Having Meng with me was very comforting. In my heart, I felt alone on this earth—no brother, no sister, no mom or dad. Now, from the Khmer Rouge, I had found a brother.

From that day on, whenever we went to fight, Meng would stay by my side. If I would turn to him and say, "Meng, I told you to stay over there," he would say, "Bun, I like to go with you, because I will protect you."

One day, we were in a tough fight. Two of my soldiers, who were packing an 81-millimeter cannon, fell down. I got mad and said, "Hey, give it to me!"

I grabbed the cannon and threw it on my shoulder and walked away. When Meng saw me do this, he came over and said, "Bun, let me carry that."

Meng and I had a lot of fun, yet we worked very hard that year. Carrying the heavy weapons and food into the jungle was hard work.

I taught Meng how to disarm and install mines, how to read the jungle, and how to listen for gunfire so he would know which way to move. I showed him how to use the B-60, a three-legged machine gun that shot a hundred rounds in less than a minute. Meng learned very quickly. Like me, he liked to fight the Khmer Rouge.

During that year, we never talked about our families. We just said, "Tomorrow we're dead anyway."

After many missions together, I went to the Big Boss and told him that I wanted Meng to be in charge of my second crew. The Big Boss told me that he trusted me, and it was up to me whether I wanted Meng to be a leader.

22 We Find Two Ladies

Missions blended into other missions. There were too many to count. It was now March 1980. After a three-day break, I once again got my crew ready and told them we would be going on another mission. As was now a custom in the Freedom Camp, the groups of people we had rescued from the cities gave us food and prayed for us as we walked away. On the first day out, I told my crew, "If we are trapped by the Khmer Rouge, don't tell them where the boss is. Just say you don't know."

Everyone understood. They also understood that we all carried one extra bullet in our sleeve pocket—if any of us were captured alive, we all knew what to do.

Two days out, I smelled something bad—the smell of dead people. I told my crew that I wanted to look around a little. Fifteen minutes later, I saw the big blue flies and walked toward them. There was a large hole, swarming with the blue flies. I saw a lot of bones there, maybe two to three hundred people, all boys and small babies. I sat at the edge of the hole to see if anybody was moving. No one was breathing down there. I called to my crew. They were angry. One of them said, "Let me go down and kill all the Khmer Rouge!"

We walked on. Not far away, we saw two people lying against a tree. They were dead. We did not know how long they had been dead, but they were like stone. Then, fifty feet away, we heard people crying. I asked one of my soldiers, "Do you hear something?"

He said, "Do ghosts cry like babies?"

We all split up to go in different directions, walking on a narrow trail. On either side were pits in the dirt made by bombs, with sharp bamboo spikes sticking out. If you fell off the trail, you were dead. Mines were all over the place. As we walked, we came upon a little kid. He was running around and looked about five years old. He had long hair, and his clothes barely hung on him. He had something hanging from his mouth, maybe some kind of weed or plant. This was a common sight in the jungle—a baby near his dead parents. At first we could not understand what was in his mouth, but soon we figured out that the babies would eat anything to stay alive: dirt, leaves, grass, and dead things. So, unlike their parents, little kids did not starve in the jungle.

I tried to catch this little kid, but he kept running. I took out some candy and tried talking to him in Cambodian and sign language. He still would not come near us. I told my crew to form a circle around him and grab him. The kid kept running from our soldiers as they closed in on him. He kept slipping away. When they finally grabbed him, he tried to bite them.

We tried to give him food, but he did not want it. We put a little candy in his mouth. Then, little by little, he ate more. I said, "This baby belongs to those parents who are dead by the tree."

After he ate a little more, he followed us. We picked him up and put him in a backpack. We walked farther up the trail, and Meng yelled to me, "Bun, there are two ladies over here."

I ran over to them and felt their heads. They were still warm. One lady had her eyes closed. Her heart was beating very slowly—one beat and a long pause. She was barely alive.

The ladies were only about fifteen or sixteen years old. I told the soldiers, "Pick them up, and put them on a sleeping hammock to carry them. Feed them water slowly." After that, I sent Meng and seven soldiers back home with the ladies and the baby. That left me with twenty-two soldiers. We kept on heading into Cambodia.

The next day, we heard a sound and saw Khmer Rouge, so we

backed up. Before long, we heard a big mine go off and then screaming and yelling. We went to look and found a lot of blood. Then we saw the green Khmer Rouge uniforms, ripped to shreds, and parts of bodies thrown around everywhere. We tried to see where the Khmer Rouge were, but we did not see any alive, only dead bodies with missing arms or legs. We backed up and went around to the village, but it was quiet. No one was around.

We went to another village. It was empty too, so we backed away. We heard a bomb behind us. My soldiers called on the radio, "The Khmer Rouge are near the food." We raced back to help the five who had remained to protect the food. When we were close, we gave the signal, shooting three times to see who would respond. Three shots came back, and we knew our crew was there.

The Khmer Rouge had fired B-60 cannons at the place where the food was. My crew had backed up after the fighting. They told me over the radio, "Don't go down there. There is a lot of bombing!"

I could hear fighting behind me. There were big and small cannons as well as gunfire. My crew called again on the radio. "The Khmer Rouge might be getting our food."

"Wait," I replied. "We are coming."

"Be very careful. There are a lot of Khmer Rouge in the area."

One of my favorite fighting tactics was called the "Water Buffalo Horn." It was called this because we would encircle the Khmer Rouge with our troops in the shape of the horns, leaving a gap at the back so the enemy could get away. We did not want to get in a firefight with the Khmer Rouge. We wanted to rescue our soldiers and get out quickly. The Water Buffalo Horn was especially effective at night.

The Water Buffalo Horn maneuver went like this: The Khmer Rouge would be in a circle in the field, with the prisoners trapped in the middle. I would sneak in at night and check the positions of their soldiers and the captured. I would then go back to my soldiers and tell them the exact positions to bomb. I would crawl back in and radio my crew to bomb behind the Khmer Rouge. The cannons would go off, and the Khmer Rouge would wake up and race over to see if their soldiers were hurt. After the Khmer had run away from us, I would take our friends back to my crew. Our soldiers would then come in from the sides, closing in on the Khmer Rouge in the shape of water buffalo horns. The Khmer soldiers would run away through the gap in the horns. This was fun. We used a good technique instead of putting our troops' lives in danger.

In this particular instance, seventeen of us went in to get our food back. Five soldiers went to the left and five to the right (about eight hundred meters apart), and they moved in using the Water Buffalo Horn tactic. We shot our guns from the sides, and then we fired our cannons at the center. The B-60 cannons told the Khmer Rouge to back away from us.

I took a couple of my soldiers in with me, and my crew bombed over my head as I gave them special instructions on the radio.

A half hour later, I went farther inside the area and told all my crew to close the gap. For a moment, the Khmer Rouge were gone. We had scared them away because they thought we were a large army. This was our trick. Seventeen of our soldiers could spread out and cover a long line so we looked like a bigger number. The Khmer Rouge always moved in close together. When they heard our guns coming from all corners, they would run away.

Now, with them scared off for a while, we took the backpacks of food and went farther into the jungle. Close to nighttime, we heard guns in front of us. We knew this was trouble now. We hid the food and went to see what it was. The sun was almost down, so we could not see clearly. Five of us went toward the sound. Soon, we heard people screaming for help. I called back to our soldiers and told them to be ready to help us. As we got closer, I said, "We have to hurry. This does not sound like Khmer Rouge. There are people who need our help."

I found a dead body, still wet with blood. I looked up and saw something moving—two kids, about seven or eight years old. When they saw me, they were afraid and started to scream. I told them, "Don't worry; we will help you."

Then we saw an adult, barely alive. My crew called me over to talk to the people who were still living and to ask them what happened.

They told us that about fifty Khmer Rouge had chased people out of the city and were killing them.

After seeing these hurt people, I got really angry—I started to sweat and felt very lightheaded. The people showed us which way the Khmer Rouge had gone. I called for ten of my crew to come quickly. The hurt people said about a hundred people, kids and adults, had come out of the city. Some of them were in good shape.

Ten of us went into the jungle to look for the people from the city who were hiding, and five of us watched for Khmer Rouge. By seven that night, we had rounded up about thirty-five people from the city. It was now dark, and we no longer heard anyone answer our calls.

That night, we told the people to sleep, but they couldn't. They wanted to find their friends and families. We told them we had to wait until morning. We gave them food and helped them with medicine. I called my crew together and told them that this terrible thing had happened because we had fought the Khmer Rouge that afternoon. They had gone back to the city and just started killing people.

By one o'clock, many of the people were sleeping, but my crew did not sleep. When the people woke up, they told us their story. They had heard the Khmer Rouge's movement before they started shooting. The Khmer Rouge told them that the Cambodian Freedom Army was outside the village. An hour later, the Khmer Rouge started bombing and shooting and burning houses. People ran out of the houses, screaming loudly, but they were killed.

About four thirty in the morning, ten of us went to the jungle to try to find more people. I found a lot of dead people, but some were still alive. We found a baby, crying and wandering around by himself. We found whole families that had been killed together, lying near their houses. The village was empty. We looked in every room, every corner, inside and outside the houses. We made a sweep of the city and saw many dead. We knew which way they had been running by which way their bodies faced.

As we went further into the village, we found seven people, kids and adults. They were alive but they had broken legs and arms. They told us to go on and showed us where more had run.

We found three more people in a hole, under the roots of a tree. We had passed that tree, but they were quiet. When we came back past the tree, they yelled to us, "Who are you?"

I said, "We are here to help."

They put their hands up in prayer and begged for their lives. "Please don't kill us."

"We will help you," I said. "Why didn't you come out when we first came by? Did you see my uniform?"

One said, "Yes, but I thought you were Khmer Rouge. When I saw you come back, I called for help. Then you saw me."

"We are the Cambodian Freedom Army," I said. "How many more are out here?" They didn't know, because they couldn't see at night, so I said, "Let's get out of this place."

They were shaking badly. When they saw my men carry the first seven out, they said, "Thank you, son. You help old people." We went back to where the first thirty-five were. They were all talking together, trying to locate the rest of their family members.

I asked them how many people lived in the village, and they explained who was missing.

I decided we had to go back to find more of them. Ten Freedom Soldiers took five village people to look in places where they knew people were hiding. The village people called out to the hidden people because their voices would be recognized.

When people saw that Cambodian Freedom Soldiers had come to help them, they got excited. One said, "My life has come back!"

The crew stayed quiet and let the people talk. We walked about two miles through the city and found fifteen dead bodies.

We did not worry about the Khmer Rouge; we knew they had run away.

After we searched through the village, we went back to where the food was hidden. We had found fifteen dead and forty-five alive. The people told us there were still forty missing who had either escaped or had been killed by the Khmer Rouge.

Now we were ready to go back to camp, where we cooked and ate together. Then we started walking toward home. We had old men, women, and the wounded to carry.

We walked for two days. On the second day, we took a break. My soldiers checked the area for two miles around us, and then we stopped and slept all night. The next morning, we talked with the people. I told them my story—how I had been starved and then rescued by the Freedom Soldiers, and how after three months of good food, I got healthy and trained very hard so that I could come back to Cambodia and help people.

One person said, "You do a good thing, Bun. You help people. You will have a long life."

The people thanked us so many times. I told them they could relax, that we were only one day away from our camp—one day away from freedom—and there would be no more danger.

We kept walking toward home. When we got close to our camp, the people came out to welcome the new ones. As soon as everyone was all taken care of, I went back to my tent.

The next morning, the Big Boss called me in. I told him about the people we saved and the ones that were hurt—how the Khmer Rouge had shot them in the village.

He went to see the wounded. Before he left, he asked me how I was doing. I said, "I'm still alive."

I walked through camp to find Meng. He was taking care of the girl by the tree who had her eyes closed and almost no pulse. He told me he had carried her back and then spent every moment with her since they got to camp. He said she was beginning to slowly recover.

She did recover, as did the other ladies we rescued.

PART THREE

Tomorrow I'm Dead

23 *A Birthday Surprise*

On my twentieth birthday, June 20, 1980, I went into Cambodia again with my number-one crew. This time we got only one day away from home before the Khmer Rouge ambushed us on the road. We were completely surrounded.

We instantly knew we were trapped. I split up the crew and then radioed Meng and his crew to come help us. They left immediately.

We saw the Khmer Rouge, and they saw us. They were scared too. By now, they knew our reputation as tough soldiers who would catch them alive.

We were in a space that was one-half mile around, and they were around the outside of us, so we had no place to go. I talked with my soldiers. Some were so scared that they had pooped their pants. They were shaking and asking me what to do.

"Don't worry," I tried to reassure them, "we will figure out what to do. Be patient. If we are killed, we will all die together. Pray for help." I called to Meng, "Give me a signal as soon as they are close to us." Then I called to my crew, "Come in closer together. There is only one road open, and our friends are coming to help us. The crew coming to relieve us will cover a day's walk in just four hours. They are carrying nothing but guns and bullets, no other supplies."

As we waited for them, we kept in radio contact with a really old radio that was carried like a backpack. It took two guys to operate.

While one spun a handle and pushed buttons, the other talked. If it was an emergency, only I talked; if it was an everyday message, anyone could talk on it.

When I saw crew number two approaching the opening in the road, twenty of us moved forward and ten stayed in the back. We started firing all our guns on the Khmer Rouge from front and back. After that, the ten in back moved out of the opening.

We went straight home after that narrow escape; we'd had enough excitement for one day. Once again, we had to throw everything down when we fought the Khmer Rouge, so we walked home with no supplies.

I went straight to the Big Boss to report. He said, "You are lucky to be alive."

"Thanks for sending crew number two to help us," I replied.

"I don't want to lose you," he said. "You are very important to me. Take a week off."

When I reported that to my crew, they jumped up and down in joy.

Khon, a crew leader, came to tell me, "Crew number three will be going into Cambodia first thing tomorrow, and everything is 100 percent set up."

When the crew walked out the next morning, I told them to call us for help if they needed it. Khon replied, "I am scared to death. I don't like to fight the Khmer Rouge, but Bun, I like to bring food for you. Without you there, I don't like to fight. That is your job!"

This made me laugh. Khon was right; I did like to fight. If I got mad, I wasn't afraid of death at all. I liked to go in and capture the Khmer Rouge alive. The more Khmer Rouge we brought out, the more food we could get for our camp.

On that day, I was very glad for a rest. I thought, *Whoa, I haven't had seven days off like this for five years!* The other soldiers took off more time than I did. I just could not do it. There were still too many people in Cambodia.

That day, I went back to relax with my soldiers and play games. Three hours later, we heard a bomb. We wondered if an animal had set it off—sometimes a monkey or a leopard was large enough to explode bombs.

I was worried because crew number three just had left; we should not have heard anything so soon. Fifteen minutes later, we heard the firing of big and small guns. I knew it wasn't right, so we set up our equipment. Then crew number three called me. "Bun, we need help! We have a fight with the Khmer Rouge!"

"How many?"

"A lot!"

Crews number one and two went to help sixty people. We did not take anything but guns, bullets, and first aid. Halfway there, we saw our crew carrying bodies. Five were hurt and were being carried back. That made me really mad. We got closer and closer, listening to the fight. We kept our radio on. I told them to make a noise and back up until we got there. When we were a half mile from crew number three, I asked how far the Khmer Rouge were from them.

"A half mile."

We set up crew number two's PG-69s, and they started shooting.

I said, "We are strong. The Khmer Rouge are sleeping in the jungle, but we have a good place to sleep." I talked like this to get us ready to fight.

We fought for one hour straight, with no one winning. The fighting was heavy. Ten of my crew members went around one side, and ten of them went around the other side. We also had crew number two's guns to fight from the front, and twenty fought from the back. I took five special soldiers with me.

I told crew number three that while they fought and made a lot of noise, we were going to sneak inside. We brought a lot of grenades with us. I told my five to go in very quietly and roll the grenades into the hole, where about a hundred Khmer Rouge were hiding. Because they were in the hole, we had trouble breaking them up with gunfire. I had crew number two stop firing the big 60 mm guns they were using, because we were inside their circle of fire. After the bombs stopped, crew two had to keep moving to avoid return fire.

We rolled the grenades down into the hole, and it got quiet. I called to crew number three to surround them and to crew number two to come around. We ordered the Khmer Rouge to drop their guns and come out, which they did.

My crew tied up their arms and took them from the area. About forty-five were alive and fifteen were dead. The rest had run away. I told crew number three, "When we came back home on this road, all was fine. This hole is fresh."

When it was clear, we looked into the hole. There were all kinds of guns in there. We took all the guns and bullets and then filled in the hole. I told the soldiers to tie rags over the Khmer Rouge's eyes so they could not see where they were going. We took them far past our camp to stay.

I asked the Khmer Rouge why they had come so close to our camp. They said they had lost many people from the city, and they were looking for them.

"We are Cambodian Freedom Soldiers," I said, "and we helped people get away from being hungry and being killed every day."

One of the Khmer Rouge said, "I just do what the boss says."

"How many of you came this way?"

"One hundred fifty came to fight and bring the people back to the city," he answered. They were young, he told me, twelve- to eighteen-year-old boys and girls. The girls were worse killers than the boys. It was said that in girls, the "red eye came up." They were angry soldiers and had the will to fight. The girls killed more than the boys.

I asked him, "What do you think right now? You are in this camp, but is this a good place for you?

He said, "No, we want to go back home."

"Right now," I said, "you need to take a break."

We took their green uniforms, put them in a pile, and burned them in front of their faces. We gave them good food and new clothes.

After that, I told them, "I am sorry about your clothes, but the Khmer Rouge are gone now—look at those ashes. No more fighting, no more sleeping in the jungle, no more walking around everywhere.

Go to sleep now and think about the past five years, from 1975 to 1980. You are with the Freedom Army now. You cannot fight. No more bullets and guns. No more green uniforms."

Some cried as I told them this.

This was the plan of the Cambodian Freedom Army. We would catch the Khmer Rouge alive and then teach them how to become good people.

I told them, "The guns and bullets have not been a friend to you. From now on, you will learn good things."

Each soldier we captured and brought back to camp gave us more proof of the fighting we were doing against the Khmer Rouge in Cambodia. We would send word to the Thailand authorities. In return, the Thai government continued to help our Freedom Camp by sending food to our soldiers and our people.

24 A Hundred More Soldiers

One morning, the Big Boss called me to a meeting. "Thank you, Bun," he said, "for helping a lot of people over the past year."

He thanked me by giving me a hundred more soldiers, who I then trained in the ways of jungle warfare. I taught them to be smart—not to just shoot but to be very quiet, shoot once, and look around. That's why we did not need a lot of people as the Khmer Rouge did—they stood together in a group and shot many rounds. My soldiers stood apart from each other in long lines and were harder to hit.

I taught my soldiers how to listen and look in the jungle. The jungle had many places to hide mines. They had to learn to be patient and read the trails, the leaves, and the trees. They had to look for disturbed soil along a trail and, at the same time, keep an eye on the trees, where an enemy might be hiding within the leaves. In the jungle, there were places where we could talk and be safe, and there were places where we had to be very quiet. Every time we stopped in the jungle, one or two soldiers walked around us to make sure we were not ambushed.

I taught them to listen to the sound of gunfire. Each gun was different. We could hear the bullets—*pow, pow, pow*. If the gunfire was low, we were to stay upright. "If they hit you in the leg, you are still alive," I told them. If the gunfire was in the middle, they were to duck down below the bullets.

"At first," I told them, "the gunfire fights will make you pee your pants. After a year, the bullets look like pieces of candy flying through the air." I would tell my soldiers, "Hey, let's go get some candy." I created animal terms to let them know what position to take in a gunfire fight. When I said "elephant," this meant we walked forward. "Crocodile" meant to get down. If I screamed "blue fly," that meant to move forward fast. We used this term when there was a pause in a fight. When the guns paused, I would yell, "Blue fly," and we would pounce on the Khmer Rouge.

I split the soldiers into three crews of thirty. Group number one would go with me into Cambodia. Number two (Meng's team) and number three were to stand by in case we needed help. We rotated the groups every two weeks. I went on every single mission. Meng was either with me or on standby. He and I could not stay in camp while we knew people still were starving and being killed out there.

My soldiers were young and fast. I told them that our job was to rescue people, not to kill. I trained them to shoot over the heads of the Khmer Rouge and scare them. They learned my yell, "Catch them alive!"

After setting up a new crew of thirty, we got ready to go back into Cambodia. Again, the people in the camp who we had rescued brought food for us to take.

After two days, we had passed all the nearby villages and were deep in the jungle and stopped at six in the evening to sleep. The next morning, we heard something close to our beds. Right away, I told five soldiers to take a look. One came back to say he'd seen three old people looking around in the jungle. We took ten soldiers, surrounded the old people, and said, "Stop!"

They had no guns, but when they put their hands up, they dropped their long knives and said, "Don't kill us!"

"We won't harm you," I said. "We are good people. Where have you come from?"

"We escaped from the Khmer Rouge in the village. There are about 250 other prisoners working for the Khmer Rouge. We came here to look for food, because once we were lucky and found a deer. Now we are hunting for monkeys."

"Are you afraid of the Khmer Rouge?" I asked.

"No, we are not."

"Well, we are the Cambodian Freedom Army."

"Where did you come from?" one asked me.

"From near the Cambodia/Thailand border."

"How many of you are there?"

"We can't tell you that information, but we have many soldiers here to help. Do you have food to eat?"

"No, we're still looking in the jungle. You won't hurt us, will you?"

"No," I repeated, "we came to help. Look at our uniforms. Will you show us the other people?"

They came with us to where we slept. When they saw the crew, the expressions on their faces changed. Their eyes sparkled. They began to smile and laugh. We gave them a little food, and then we sat to talk.

Then I asked one to show me the others still in the village, and he did.

Not far away, we saw people inside a shelter made of bamboo. Some were asleep; some were watching us, afraid and shaking.

The old women and old men said, "Don't kill us."

"Don't worry," I said. "We are here to help you." I asked if the Khmer Rouge had come by here.

"No, not at this time of year," one answered.

We gave them food and showed them how to eat slowly. We gave first aid to some sick people. I called Meng on the radio to tell him we had found people.

When the people heard me telling crew number two to bring more food, they were very happy to know we had lots of help.

I told the people that we needed to leave this place to go back toward crew number two. "Some of you will have to help our soldiers carry the sick," I said.

We met up with crew number two the next day. Meng took over

to make sure all the people got back to our camp safely. Before they left, we took some food from crew number two to take with us back to Cambodia. Then we told the people to go with the crew to the safe camp. They all thanked us, and different ones told us we were doing a good thing by saving all these people and that we would all have long lives. Several people said, "We will pray for you."

25 No Gun, No Life

We returned to the jungle every week to fight the Khmer Rouge and rescue people. It was now 1981. We would send five special scouts out ahead of us to look for enemy soldier positions. Then we would decide where to go.

On one mission, when we got to a new village, we immediately knew something was not right. The Khmer Rouge were patrolling the outskirts of the village—they were waiting for us. We opened fire and fought with them for three hours that night.

Right away, I called crew number three to say we had fought a lot of Khmer Rouge, and I did not know how long our food would last. Crew number three took off right away and radioed every hour to check in. We shot at the Khmer Rouge every once in a while, just to let them know we were still there, defending ourselves.

At four in the morning, we went into the jungle to hide and sleep. In the early morning, while we were still sleeping, the Khmer Rouge came to "clean our faces," meaning we had no time to wash our faces but had to jump up and run with nothing. They did not see us; they just came close, shooting as they ran. None of our crew was hit. We did a lot of running that day, straight toward camp.

At noon, we met up with crew number three, which was coming to bring us food and supplies. As we ate together, I said, "Let's go back to camp and forget this."

Crew number three gave us some bullets, but we had to leave everything else behind—food, hammocks, clothes, and backpacks. Our guns, however, never left our arms. They were locked to us at all times, even when we were sleeping and eating. If you had no gun, you had no life.

Back home, I checked on all the people and asked how the babies and children were. The next day, I went to see the Big Boss. I told him that all our supplies had been left in the jungle. He said, "Don't worry; you are alive." He gave us brand new equipment.

After a little break, we went down again. This time I took sixty soldiers with me. We walked for three days into Cambodia and found two small camps of people who were hiding in the jungle. There were about three hundred of them. We split up into two crews, one for each camp, and took them away. We gave them food, talked with them, and told them who we were until they trusted us. We took them with us that night, carrying those who couldn't walk. We slept a little bit at midnight and then went for two days straight without stopping, until we reached the border.

People under the Khmer Rouge in the village were like dogs, cowering and afraid; but once trained and in the jungle, they were tigers—mean and no longer afraid. They made bows and arrows to fight the Khmer Rouge.

After that mission, it became harder to go to the village to rescue people. The Khmer Rouge were everywhere; they had seen too many Cambodian Freedom Fighters get people out.

On one patrol, we walked two days until we were deep in Khmer Rouge territory. Once again, our job was to fight with the Khmer Rouge and try to rescue people who were still trapped in the cities. We got to the city and found that we could do nothing for anyone, so we headed back to camp.

We were in the jungle, heading away from Khmer Rouge territory. There were many roads in the jungle, and all of them were mined with bombs. I told my crew to follow behind me, and I would clean out our road, making sure there were no mines. As I walked down the road, my crew walked about ten feet behind me.

I carefully removed twenty Chinese mines. These mines were easy to see, as there were strings crossing the road. All I had to do was look under a leaf on the ground and take the clip off the bomb.

I looked farther down the road and saw many more strings. "Whoa!" I said to my crew. "Too many strings!"

As I was looking ahead at all these Chinese mines, I stepped down and felt metal prongs compress under my foot.

"Oh oh!" I said, turning to my soldier friend Khon. "I just stepped on a big one."

"How big?" he asked.

"A 69."

"Whoa!"

I told my soldiers to come over and dig a hole for me. As I stood, there the pins of the 69 mine kept lifting up. Each time they did, I would step down harder to keep the bomb from going off. Khon and my crew grabbed a small shovel and started to dig a hole next to me. If the bomb went off, we were all dead.

In five minutes, they had a hole big enough for me to fall in. They put plugs in my ears and nose, wrapped up my eyes, and left me there next to the hole, with the 69 bomb pulsing below my foot. The crew went back thirty-five feet and ducked down on the ground.

As soon as they were clear, I counted, "One … two … three," whipped my foot off the prongs, and jumped in the hole as fast as I could.

The bomb shot five feet in the air and exploded thirty feet around. All the small trees and vegetation around me were blasted away.

My crew ran back to me very fast and dragged me out of the small hole. Half of my uniform had been burned off my body, and my skin was burned on that side, but I was still alive.

I was unconscious for forty-five minutes. When I woke up, I didn't remember what had happened; I only knew there was a lot of blood and burns on one side of my body.

My soldiers carried me back, and we decided to go in a different direction. I was very sore and couldn't hear. My soldiers offered to carry me further, but I told them I would walk, although I walked slowly. We walked all day, but kept going. The next day we finally reached the Freedom Camp.

I went to the Big Boss and told him what had happened—my crew had later reminded me. I told him how Khon and the crew had dug the hole for me and saved my life and that no one was hurt except for me.

"There are too many bombs now," he said. "Be careful out there."

"I'd like to put Khon in charge of crew number three," I said. "He is a good soldier and I trust him."

The Big Boss looked at me—at my wounds and my burns—and said, "The decision is up to you."

26 *The Special Force*

I reported to the Big Boss and said, "We are already changing the Khmer Rouge into Cambodian Freedom Fighters." Then I said that I wanted to get the five dead from our crew and cremate them. This way, their spirits could be released from the physical bodies faster to find new babies and new lives to be born into.

I called to the ninety-five of my crew who were left to stand in a line. We shot our guns to salute the dead as a memorial for them. We told stories of each one before we put him on the fire. Thirty of the older Cambodian people came to watch the fire and make sure it all burned. When they took over, all the soldiers went back home. Then people played games around the bodies on the fire all day and night, another custom in our country.

The next morning, the Big Boss called me and the leaders of my crews to a meeting. There were already five hundred soldiers lined up when we arrived. I wondered what they were doing there.

The Big Boss told the soldiers that I had been in charge of all three crews and that I had lost five from the hundred men. The Big Boss was giving a punishment to me and my crew leaders to teach us a lesson. He said to all the soldiers, "All of you, do not learn to do like Bun's crew did. Five of their people are dead."

Then, as punishment, he had me do three hundred push-ups, and he had the crew leaders do one hundred push-ups. All five hundred soldiers watched. We were done very quickly and then went back to our camp.

I met with the crew leaders and asked if they were okay. They said they weren't okay, but I joked, "Hey, I can do three hundred more. Next time we get in trouble, we will do double!" This was the first time I had been punished, and I thought, *I do ninety-nine things right and one thing wrong, and for that one thing I get a punishment.*

My crew leaders and I discussed how we could do better from now on. I was angry at myself that day. I went home to sleep, trying to figure out how to do more to save my soldiers. We wanted to keep the blood inside our bodies, not on the outside.

The next morning, I made my own sign. It read "Tomorrow I'm Dead."

I wrote this and drew a skull and crossbones on paper and went around asking people if it was a good symbol for my clothes. Most people said it was good because our crew stood by twenty-four hours a day, ready to help, not afraid to die.

I showed my Big Boss, and he said it was good. Before this time, my crew had been regular soldiers, but now he gave me a group that would be ready to help any other crew that needed us. My crew was made up of only the best soldiers. We were named the "Special Freedom Force."

If we were needed, we had to go, no question, eight days a week and twenty-five hours a day. I left my boss and went back to my crew to show them the new sign. They all liked it and wanted one on their shirts. I also told them the Big Boss had named us the "Special Freedom Force."

They all yelled and screamed, "Special Freedom Force? Does that mean we will have to stay in Cambodia?"

I said, "No, we will help all the crews now."

Everybody was excited and said, "Hey! We are heroes now! We are number one! We are at the top now!"

We ordered clothes for one hundred, with my sign embroidered on them. Our uniforms were a slightly different color than the others, still camouflage but a little brighter tone.

More young soldiers were sent to me for training. I taught them how to be good soldiers, how to rescue people, and how to stay alive in the jungle. When I went on a rescue, I took the stripes off my sleeve. (One received a stripe for every one hundred soldiers under his command. I had three stripes.) If we were captured and asked who was in charge, we would say we didn't know. We each had one bullet in our pockets for just such an occasion. We knew that if the Khmer caught us, they would string our arms up in trees and cut us, trying to get us to talk. Each question brought more cuts, until you were dead. Sometimes the Khmer pulled your fingernails out, one by one, day by day, unless you talked. We knew we would never talk if captured, so instead of enduring the torture, we had one spare bullet to use on ourselves.

Despite the dangers, I was happy that year. We were young, full of energy, and had no responsibilities except staying alive, and we were confident in our own abilities. Once, while on a rescue, we had been walking into Cambodia for two days when we heard gunfire ahead. We kept walking for a half hour and then sent two new soldiers ahead to take a look. When they returned, they reported that they'd seen round hats. They had not seen hats like this before.

We moved on and saw a couple of Vietnamese tanks roll by. The Vietnamese were fighting the Khmer Rouge! I said to my soldiers, "Back up; that's a big bullet!"

Before long, the Vietnamese saw some of us and shot that huge gun at us. They didn't know we were on their side. Trees shattered everywhere. Another bomb exploded against a tree, and a big piece of shrapnel hit my head.

One of my crew said, "Brother, I see water coming from your head." We never said "blood."

I felt numb and asked how big my wound was. He told me the skin had come off my forehead.

My crew bandaged my forehead, and when that was done, I looked around. It was very quiet. Our guns were pointed in every direction to protect us. We did not try to fight back; we just tried to stay away from the Vietnamese.

We started walking back. An hour later, we came upon the Khmer Rouge who were running from the Vietnamese. We fought with them for about ten minutes, and then I told my crew, "Let's go the other way." It was like we were playing hide-and-seek with both the Khmer Rouge and the Vietnamese. The Khmer Rouge ran one way, and we ran another way.

As it was almost night, we looked for a safe place to take a break and soon found a spot on a small hill, where we could see in all directions. I radioed home and said, "We had some fun today. We saw both Khmer Rouge and Vietnamese."

We took a break, and I told my crew, "When I sleep, you watch. When you sleep, I watch. Don't worry; be happy."

Soon we heard a very loud noise. It sounded like a tree had collapsed. The soldiers on guard were scared to death, thinking the Vietnamese army was coming. We went in closer to the sound and heard screaming.

Then we saw two giant elephant butts—two elephants scratching their backsides on trees. I said, "Don't worry; the kings are here. Those tanks cannot run over these elephants."

We sat up all night, watching the elephants, to make sure they didn't run us over. Nobody got any sleep that night. Most of the time when we saw animals in the jungle, we were happy. I would tell my soldiers, "More power. Elephants are smarter than people; they run from danger."

First we prayed for the elephants—"Good luck to you. Be careful. Don't meet with a bullet"—and then we retreated at about five in the morning, on a different route into Cambodia.

My crew was a fun group in the jungle, while looking for friends or enemies. They liked to hike and were not afraid to fight.

I had become used to life in the jungle. I had made friends with the snakes, wild animals, and insects. If my crew saw a snake, they would call me, and I would catch it alive. All animals were my friends.

The weather had become hot and dry. Even the jungle was now dry. This was good for us, because it meant the leeches were gone. To protect ourselves from biting insects, we wore gloves and wrapped up our heads at night while we slept.

One day, we saw another crew of Cambodian Freedom Soldiers who were looking to rescue people. We told them we had seen Khmer Rouge and Vietnamese soldiers; they told us they had not seen them.

We were happy to see these guys; it gave us more power. We talked about getting people out of a city that was one day's walk away. Both crews went together. There were sixty of us in all. When we got to the city, the other crew went in first. Their leader and I were talking when one of their crew stepped on a mine. The Vietnamese heard the explosion and came looking for us, still unaware we were all fighting against the Khmer Rouge.

We split up the crew that was left and started shooting warning shots at the Vietnamese. I told my crew to keep their eyes on the ground. One mine had gone off, and there might be more. The Vietnamese started firing heavily at us. I sent five soldiers to go around the back, and we all fired on the Vietnamese to slow them down.

The Vietnamese raised a white cloth in surrender. I told my men to be careful; they might be tricking us. We raised a white cloth too. I stood behind a big tree, waved my hat, and yelled, "We are the Cambodian Freedom Army, not Khmer Rouge!" I stepped out from behind the tree and showed them my uniform. "Cambodian Freedom! We have no fight with you. We came to help people."

While I was talking, the Vietnamese came around behind us, and my crew started shooting at them. They shot back. We split up and ran in all directions. It took us about an hour to find each other again. No one was hurt. I said, "The Vietnamese were playing a game with us. They held out a white cloth but then sent soldiers behind us."

The next morning, I asked if anyone was scared. When they all said yes, I said, "Let's go home. At least now we know the Vietnamese are here to help."

Once we were home, I described the Vietnamese uniforms to our soldiers—blue, with a blue round hat. Then I showed them my forehead. I joked, "I guess I had too much skin so they took some off."

We met with all our people, and I told them that we had seen the Vietnamese. "They had big tanks, and they fought hard. We ran all around the jungle to get away from their big guns. Then we saw big elephants, scratching their butts."

My crew tried to rest, but about two hours later, the front line ran into camp to say that the Vietnamese were coming close—right now! I jumped up and told crews one and two that it was time to go. There were sixty of us. We grabbed guns and bullets. The enemy was not far away. The closer we got to the front line, the louder the noise was.

We split into groups of ten to surround the front line. We fought on the back of the line first and then moved forward. We used a lot of our big bombs and scared them. When it was quiet, we could hear screaming. People called to us in Cambodian. "Don't kill us!"

I said, "Let me see your hands!"

They dropped their guns, put their hands up, and came to us. I asked how many there were and why they were here. He said, "Only fifteen." Their leader had seen our Cambodian Freedom Army. They had come looking for us and Khmer Rouge.

We tied them up and blindfolded them all night. When we returned, people from camp came to look at them. Now we had evidence of Vietnamese.

The Big Boss called the Thailand authorities to come down. We sent the Vietnamese to Thailand because we had no jail in the camp for them. We took their weapons, which were really old handguns, including M-16s and AK-47s. All they had with them were guns and clothes.

We slept there on the front line, making friends with the other front line soldiers we had captured. They were scared to death from the fight. They had three rounds in their guns; we had 120 rounds. We stayed with them all night, and in the morning, we went back home.

At home, the Big Boss came to help us. I thanked him for the front line's being very fast; otherwise, we would not have been able to help. Once again, a small crew was better against a big one. We could easily spread out and cover each other.

In the morning, back at camp, the people came to ask us what had happened the night before. My crew told them stories. Everyone listened with big eyes. "The Vietnamese are here?" someone asked.

Later, I called a meeting and said to my crew, "Thank you. We got the job done really quickly, and nobody was hurt. This is our house. We don't want anybody to burn our house, right?"

"Right!"

"There is a ring around us. We don't want anybody inside that ring. That's all we have. We have no place else to go. The Khmer Rouge does not even know about it."

Then the Big Boss called all the leaders to a secret meeting. We were a little scared that the Vietnamese were inside our ring. Before, we'd had one front line; now, we made a second one, farther away. We had more people now who had been rescued and had joined our army. The outer line would call in to us if the enemy came, and they would start fighting. The second line protected them, and we would be on call. I told the Big Boss that I needed to place some mines outside our circle to stop them; otherwise, it was too easy for them to get us. If we heard one mine go off, we could go out right away.

Finally, everything was set up to protect our jungle camp. We were ready to go back into Cambodia.

That day, the Big Boss told everyone that I would be in charge of two hundred soldiers. He told me, "Bun, you will have another hundred for your crew."

I told him that I would have to handpick my soldiers again. I gathered all the soldiers in camp, walked up to each kid, and asked him if he had any family. If he had family still alive, I told him that he could not go with me. Our crew was special—orphans only on twenty-four-hour standby, ready to fight at any time; it didn't matter when. If we were killed, we all knew that no one would cry.

I set up all the soldiers and split up my crew. The old members of my crew trained the new members. After we trained, we took the crew to the jungle and practiced jungle warfare. The new crew were scared of the jungle, but I told them that we had all these "old" soldiers (seventeen to eighteen years old) to learn from. I told them to watch them and do what they did.

The next week, we took half of the new crew down to find Khmer Rouge. All along the way, we taught them how to fight. We were very lucky that day and came upon more than one hundred Khmer Rouge. We set up in the woods and told the new soldiers what to do.

We were spread out, with about twenty feet between each soldier. On either end of our line were veteran soldiers with radios. We stayed in contact as we swept in, formed like a crescent shape, firing our guns and closing in from the outside while we screamed, "Catch them alive!"

Inside that sweeping half circle, the Khmer Rouge shot back and then started to run away. Those who saw they could not escape dropped their guns.

I put the new soldiers in charge of the captured Khmer Rouge. Most were only thirteen and fourteen years old.

I told my crew, "That is it for today." As we walked back to camp, I asked my new kids, "How are you doing?"

"We're scared to death."

"The first time is always the worst," I reassured them. "My first time, when I heard guns and bullets, I peed my pants, and some of the other soldiers had pooped themselves. We too had been scared by the bullets and explosions. This is normal. After fighting a long time, bullets coming at us looked like candy. You, too, will find 'candy' in the jungle."

When we got back to camp, we got a distress call from Meng and crew number two. They had gone out on a patrol and gotten in a fight with some Vietnamese soldiers.

I called him and asked how far away they were. He said two days. I told him to keep an eye on the Vietnamese and back up toward our camp. I sent Khon and crew three to help out. They were told to move fast, but by the time crew three had reached our soldiers, the game was over. There was no more fighting, so they headed home.

There seemed to be no strategic plan for defeating the Khmer

Rouge. The Freedom Army was too weak to do more than just rescue people from the Khmer Rouge.

After one week of rest in camp, we headed out on another mission. I had told the Big Boss that we needed to go to different villages farther away. All the villages close to us were empty of people. I told him the Vietnamese in 1979 were entering the cities and villages and trying to take control. They did not know who we were and thought we were a danger to them. He told me to take more soldiers on the next mission and to be careful.

The next time, I took one hundred soldiers and more food and bullets. We walked for a day and came upon a huge river. The opposite bank was at least half a mile away, and the water was deep. We started chopping down banana and coconut trees to make rafts. We lashed together all the wood that would float. We had to get our guns, cannons, and food on these rafts. There was no way to swim this river, carrying our weapons. We waited until night to make sure the Khmer Rouge or Vietnamese would not see us in the water.

Once it got dark, we took off into the water. We flashed our lights ahead and could see green and red eyes staring back at us, all over the water—to our left and to our right, ahead, and behind. Coming toward us were these very large eyes, the eyes of a crocodile.

We knew that crocodiles could kill us only if we were on top of the water. Underneath the surface, they were our friend. We could swim with them and touch them, because they could not bite us underwater.

My troops took Chinese bombs and swam under the water toward the crocodile. When they got close to the crocodile, they dove underwater, dropped the bomb on the bottom, and then swam back toward our crew, holding the strings to the bombs. Once my crew were on the surface again, they pulled the strings. The explosion scared the snakes and crocodile out of our path. We paddled our rafts across the river, toward the other bank.

When we were safely across, we took a break. We were now in Vietnamese territory. We could see their lights. I snuck into their camp to see how many soldiers there were and how big their guns were. They had many big guns and many soldiers. I went back to my crew, and at ten that night, we opened fire with our cannons. For fifteen minutes, we shot at the village. After that we invaded their camp, but all the Vietnamese had run away. We cleaned up our equipment and then moved out fast. We could hear guns shooting back at us.

In the distance, a tank's long-arm cannon went off. There was an explosion in the jungle where the bombs landed. It looked like lightning. The bombs didn't scare us. We had been through so much war by this point that these sounds did not bother us anymore. My kids liked fighting at night because the bombs and bullets looked like fireworks in the sky.

We moved out, far away from the bombs. We lay down behind trees to take a break until morning, when we decided to walk back home. We were nearly out of food and bullets. The trip had taken us four days, but it took just two days to get back to camp.

On the way, we looked for the stashes of Khmer loot. I would find gold jewelry and put it in a gallon can I kept in my room. The can was getting full from all the trips to fight the Khmer Rouge. I knew one day I would be able to do something good with all of the money from this gold.

That night I stayed with soldiers on the second line. I was asleep when one of my crew ran into me on his way downhill to get water for cooking. When he told me he was going to the river, I said, "Wait— let me go. There are many mines down there. Walk behind me." I moved very carefully down the trail, trying to feel my way in the dark. Suddenly, I felt a string on my leg. I carefully followed it to the Chinese mine and disarmed it.

I moved a bit farther and found another. This went on for part of an hour. We got close to the river, but I could not see a thing. I could not remember the exact spot where I had stuck the next mine. I took another step in the dark and felt the string move on my leg. I jumped for the ground as the mine blasted off with a huge explosion. Luckily,

I had pointed the mine down the trail toward the Khmer Rouge and away from us. I was hit by fire and hot air but not by the bomb. My uniform was badly burned and my hair was singed. The kid behind me had burned hair too. The bomb had woken up the entire camp.

Within a minute, my entire Special Force came running down the hill, half dressed, to find out what had happened.

My soldiers knew that a mine going off could only mean one of two very bad things: either enemy soldiers were at our camp, or one of our own soldiers had stepped on a mine.

If the Khmer Rouge or Vietnamese heard a mine go off, they immediately would launch cannon fire directly at the spot the explosion came from. This is why my soldiers showed up half dressed—they knew they needed to get our soldiers out of there fast.

When they saw me and asked what had happened, I explained that it was so dark, I had lost track of the mines and accidentally broken a string.

We all laughed. Now, at least we knew that our mines were pointed at the Khmer Rouge and not at our own soldiers.

27   *Buddha Will Smile*

The next day, our second-line soldiers wished us luck as we took off on another mission. We passed through the mines and got into the jungle one day later.

At dawn the next morning, we were ready to go again. My crew walked until midday and took a break for fifteen minutes. Two of my crew went to look around. They saw a big hole, and upon getting closer, they saw thousands of blue flies. Then they saw that hundreds of dead filled the hole. We all walked to the hole and looked in to see if any of the people were still alive. It seemed like the Khmer Rouge had brought a whole city out and dumped them in the hole. The bodies were all swollen; we could not recognize anyone, so we went forward.

We saw people running across the field again, so we watched which way they went. There were about a hundred of them. We tried to stop them, but they were afraid of us, so we ran out in front of them, and I said, "Don't worry; we are good people. We won't hurt you. Look at our uniforms. We are the Cambodian Freedom Army. We know that the Vietnamese came to hurt people. Don't run; you are safe now. I will drop my gun, so you will believe me. Sit down with us."

All of them came out. The people stopped running and gathered around me. They said they were running from the Khmer Rouge.

It was hard to recognize them as people; they were so skinny and ragged. I talked with one older lady. She told me, "I have a family, but I couldn't feed them. We had no food." I hugged her and cried really hard. All I could feel in my arms was skin and bones. I called her Mom.

The lady told me that the Vietnamese had come in and started killing people in the city, so they ran to the jungle. They were scared and ate anything they could find.

I told myself that I had to help these families; I had to get them out fast. I told my soldiers that they had to take good care of these people. They agreed, saying, "Yes, my brother."

I sent some soldiers to look a half mile around that place to make sure no one was around. We took out bags of food for the people. Immediately, some ladies started to fight over the food. I told them, "Take it easy. We have more."

Then we cried together again. These were humans, not animals. We opened more backpacks of food. They ate and drank water. They thanked us repeatedly. They said that sometimes they saw people in the jungle and would ask them if they had found food, but they could not go back to the city.

We could hear guns far away. I asked if they heard the guns often, and they said, "Yes, every day."

Then we heard guns close to us. The people wanted to run, but I told them to stay with me and I'd protect them. I sent ten soldiers toward the sound of the guns, and when they saw this, the people calmed down a little. They had been scared for so many days. After that, we took them away from the bombs. My soldiers wanted me to call crew number two for help, but I said, "No, we will take care of this. We're only two days from home." When we were at a safe distance, we called the ten soldiers to come back to us.

About a hundred people were with us. When we were one day away from camp, we stopped to eat and sleep. I decided to call crew number two to pick up the people and bring more food, double the usual amount.

Crew two showed up a day later. The people were so happy to see so many soldiers. I took half the food with me to go back and find more people, while crew number two took these people home. My crew was happy they had helped so many, and they wanted to find more people.

Some said they could find people all by themselves—they all joked with each other. They wanted to find more people because it made them happy. When we gathered together that day, we held hands and prayed that if our parents were alive in the jungle, lost or running from the Khmer Rouge, someone would help them, like we helped these people.

Two days later, we came close to a city and heard tanks. We hid from them, but the Khmer Rouge came up behind us, and we started fighting with them.

When the Vietnamese heard this, they began to bomb us. My crew didn't know what to do. I said to stop fighting and be really quiet, but the cannon fire kept coming. Bombs were making huge holes all around us. I told my soldiers to go to a big hole where they could keep an eye on the Khmer Rouge and wait until we could escape. They stayed at the edge of the hole and shot at anyone who came close. I knew this would last all day. Big cannons and small guns were firing. The tanks could not come in the jungle, but they had a long arm that could reach us, so we waited.

I thought, *Should I call crew two or three on the radio? Or wait a while until it's quiet and try to get out?*

My leaders wanted me to call for help, but I said, "They are two days away. How could they help? We don't even know where the enemies are. Please, just be quiet and listen to me."

My soldiers heard two Khmer Rouge crawling toward our hole, so we were quiet and waited and watched. They had no guns. I yelled at them, "Who are you?"

They could not walk, because their legs were broken from the bullets. They pleaded with us not to kill them. Four of my men dragged them into the hole. They begged for water. I thought it was likely that one of my men had shot them earlier that day. One had lost his leg. Only ragged meat hung from it, so we just cut it off and wrapped it.

Again they begged for water. We gave them some, but not too much, because too much would kill them. We soaked rags in the water and dripped it into their mouths. They thanked us.

I figured they had come near us to get away from the Vietnamese. "You are lucky," I said, "even though you don't have a leg. At least you will see your family again."

I asked them if they had heard of Cambodian Freedom Fighters. They had heard of us but said they did not like our side.

"We help people," I told them. "You are lucky we found you. We will take you to our camp and give you good food and good sleep. Your side just leaves people for dead. I never leave my crew. They are special; they help people. Khmer Rouge have killed millions of people. I catch Khmer Rouge alive, but I don't kill them."

These kids started to cry and lifted their hands up to their faces for forgiveness. "We are sorry," one said. "We are on the wrong side."

We left the hole and got away from the reach of the long-armed tank. An hour later, we stopped to sleep while two of our crew watched. The next morning, I decided we would go back home. We were tired. We carried the wounded Khmer Rouge with us. When we approached our outer ring, we shot three times. A half hour later, we came to the group on the outer ring, and I said, "I have two Khmer Rouge with me."

"Okay," one said, "I'll eat them alive."

"Okay, whatever you want."

We passed the inner ring to our camp, but took the Khmer Rouge around the outside to our warehouse. We had to watch them every second to protect them from the people in the camp. Someone at the camp asked, "The Khmer Rouge look like that?" Others shouted at them, throwing rocks and sticks. "You killed my mother, father, brother, sister. Join our side, or we will eat you."

The people told me that I was too nice to the Khmer Rouge. I told them, "The Khmer Rouge look like me—two eyes, two legs, and human hearts pumping blood. If you do bad to people, bad comes back to you."

One soldier said, "Bun, it's good that I am not a leader like you. If I was the leader, I would kill them all."

I visited awhile with the people who had been running away from the Khmer Rouge. When you are a leader, people always come to you for everything. They all knew me. When they asked me how I was, I told them, "There are a lot of drums out there, and pigs came to see me."

They knew what I was saying. Drums were bombs, and pigs were the Khmer Rouge. They asked me where the pigs were, and I said, "You can go see them over there." That night we sang, danced, told jokes, and had fun.

A lot of women asked to wash my crew's clothes, and we watched them wash our clothes in the river, lathering and rinsing. They brought the clothes back to hang out to dry behind the house. Then they ironed the clothes and put them in buckets for us. When we met to play games, we thanked them for cleaning our clothes. We would say, "All those ladies are like our sisters."

Some of the ladies liked me, but I told them, "All I want are sisters, not a wife right now."

I knew that my soldiers looked up to me and watched how I behaved. I had to be good to all people, including the nice ladies in camp. When my clothes wore out, the ladies would clean them very gently, but they would tell me to get new ones. But I said, "No, I like my old clothes."

They would laugh at me. I liked to wear my clothes until they were gone.

My soldiers and I would tease each other at camp, saying things like, "Hey, that lady likes you," or "That skinny one likes you," or "Two of them like you."

I would say, "They are our sisters. If I find my parents, sister, and brothers, they will take over and find a wife for me. That is the Cambodian way."

The next morning, I told the Big Boss that I needed to take a week's break. This was the first time since gaining freedom from the Khmer Rouge that I had asked for a break. I had been on missions constantly since then. He answered, "Good for you."

When I told my crew they had a break for a week, they jumped out of bed, screaming and yelling. They said, "Let's go over and see how Meng's crew number two and Khon's crew number three are doing!"

We visited crew number two first. I hid behind my crew as they walked in. Crew number two saw us come in and said, "Oh no, not again!"—they thought we were calling on them again. One of my crew said to them, "You gotta get up! They need you on the front line!"

They all dropped everything and started packing up in a hurry. They lined up in three rows of ten. My crew said, "Hey, you are missing a button" and "Hey, you need to shine your shoes! Fix it before our boss comes!"

Then I turned around from where I was hiding and laughed. I pulled the crew leader aside and said, "My kids scared your kids. Go tell them to drop their guns and go to bed."

He said, "One, two, three—put down your guns and go to bed."

They all looked at each other and said, "Huh?" Then my crew broke out in laughter. Crew number two ran over to jump on them and fight with them, shouting, "You really scared us!"

They wrestled around. My soldiers always joked with each other like this when they were not fighting.

That night I got all three hundred of my soldiers together and gave them some advice. I said, "Be careful. Don't hurt anyone, because it will turn back on you, and then the bullet will find you. Don't even break the limb of a tree when you take a rest in the jungle. It hurts the plant, just as if I were to reach out and break your finger. Don't hurt people or even yell at them. Buddha will smile on you. If you are good, people will like you, and you will live longer.

"Respect your parents first, because they raised you. Then respect Buddha, trees, mountains, and everything. It is not a rule, but it is a way to live your life. If you get in trouble, grab some dirt, put it on your head, and pray, 'Dirt, please help me.' We grow from the dirt, and we go back to the dirt. In an emergency, the dirt will help you stay alive.

"Do not spit, piss, or poop in the water; it is life, and it keeps moving. Without it, you have no life. Be honest. If you want to see your mother, father, brother, sister, or uncle again, you must be straight in your life. If you don't believe me, maybe you will see for yourself."

After my speech I said good night and went back to my tent.

28 *The Teacher*

One night in October 1982, I dreamed about a gunfire fight that would not stop. When I woke up, I was very troubled. I went to talk with one of the families in the camp. They invited me in to eat breakfast. The daughter cooked for us, and as we ate and visited, I asked how the new people were coming along. They said, "Pretty good."

I told them I needed to see another family, so I left their house and started walking down the street. I was walking by a small bamboo house with a leaf roof. The old man, Ta Sorm, who had witnessed my blood-brother ceremony, was sitting on the front porch. He had white hair, his skin was wrinkled, and he was very thin. He called me by name and asked me to come over.

He told me he knew all about the brave work I was doing. He said he was one of the ten thousand people my crew had saved from the Khmer Rouge. He knew that I had to run around and take care of my soldiers, running back and forth in the jungle to save people and running to fight the Khmer Rouge and Vietnamese. Then he asked me if I had an hour to spare.

He told me he had seen me go off to fight many times. "Do you want more power?" he asked.

"I have plenty of energy when I eat good food," I replied.

He said, "No, power from God, a letter from Buddha."

"What kind of letter?"

"A letter to wear on your body."

I said, "Okay, I would like that." I was thinking I would get a piece of paper with the letter on it.

"Take off your shirt and your long pants," he instructed me. He took out a long stick with three needles poking out from it. He had black ink in a pan. "I'll give you three things to help you. First, for when you go on the front line, this letter will help you sound more than 110 percent louder when you are yelling. The second is for animal bites. If a snake tries to bite you, day or night, this letter will help you. It will protect you from bombs also. Third is to help you run fast and never get tired. That's what I want to give you. I do this because when I look at you, you look like my son. I've never given these letters to anybody before."

Then he took the stick, poked it in the ink, and then poked it on my neck. "That's the first one, for yelling loud and strong." The second tattoo went on my ankle. "That's protection from animal bites—spiders, crocodiles, snakes, and all animals on the ground." The final tattoo went on both knees. "That's the Buddha letter for running fast."

The tattoos hurt, but I did not say anything. The old man had found me and wanted to help keep me alive. I hoped that the letters would help me.

The next time we went to Cambodia to fight, the Khmer Rouge attacked us right away. We split up to make it hard to shoot us. My soldiers were thirty feet apart, again using our Water Buffalo Horn maneuver. We set up for the fight and our soldiers at the ends started shooting. I was in the middle and yelled, "Let's go! Catch them alive!"

The soldiers on the end raced in, shooting their guns in the air and scaring away the Khmer Rouge. After the Khmer Rouge were gone, my soldiers came back to me. One said, "Bun, your voice is really loud. We can hear you much better than before."

I told them about the old man and showed the tattoo on my neck that made my voice loud. Then I showed them the tattoos on my ankle and on my knees. I explained what they were for. They all wanted tattoos just like mine.

"When we get home," I told them, "I will show you where to go." I didn't tell them that they could not ask the old man teacher for anything; he would come to them.

We fought many missions after that. On every trip home, we would try to swing by the Khmer Rouge stash of loot and pick up some more jewelry.

After one of these missions, in 1983, I went to my tent, carrying a gold necklace, rings, and watches from the jungle. I walked over to my cans and saw a letter on my bed. I didn't think it was important—I always got letters—but this one had no return address. I put away my jewelry and set down my backpack. Finally, I walked to my bed. I picked up the letter and tore it open.

It was from my mom!

PART FOUR

My Mom Finds Me

29 *My Parents' Escape*

My mom wrote me from a Thai refugee camp. The letter said she had been writing the United Nations Red Cross Refugee Camps since 1979, asking the authorities if they had seen her son.

During the 1975 Khmer Rouge takeover, older people and babies were kept in the cities to do menial work and build equipment for the laborers in the Killing Fields. Only the children and teenagers were sent to the fields.

After four years as a slave, making equipment for the young workers in the rice fields, my dad awoke to the sound of heavy bombing. My parents thought that maybe the Khmer Rouge were fighting each other. For hour after hour, the bombs never stopped. My dad said, "What is going on out there? Where do the bombs come from?"

They walked two miles away from the city, with the terrible bombing and noise everywhere around them. They came to a place by a wide, deep river, where they could see tanks and soldiers on the other side.

"Whoa, that is not Khmer Rouge; that is Vietnamese."

The two armies were fighting each other. After a while, the bombing stopped. My dad watched the Vietnamese soldiers swimming across the river toward the Khmer Rouge side. Cambodian people on the riverbank saw this and realized they could get to the

Vietnamese side and freedom if they swam. They started swimming across the wide brown river.

Thousands of people got in the river. The Khmer Rouge soon found this out and started bombing the river. The Vietnamese started bombing the Khmer Rouge.

My father cut down banana trees and made a small raft. He grabbed my mom and little brother and put them on top of the raft. My mom could not swim. He then ran out into the water. The Vietnamese were screaming on loud speakers from the other side to hurry up. My father kicked in the water, trying to get the raft across the wide river. Bullets whizzed by his ear, and bombs exploded in the water. Many people were killed. The water began to turn red. The current pushed my father downstream into the thick of the bullets and bombs, but people came out into the river to help him push the raft toward the bank. Somehow, my parents and brother escaped.

The Vietnamese soldiers told them to run away from this terrible place and that the UN Red Cross trucks were waiting on a road about two miles away. They made it to the trucks and got in. My parents were taken to a refugee camp in a special part of Thailand.

After a short time in camp, my parents went to the Red Cross and told them that they wanted to go my father's original home in Thailand. They had worked and lived in Cambodia to make money, but he and my mom were Thai citizens. The Red Cross asked them for their identification, but this had been taken and burned by the Khmer Rouge. My father asked the Thai people to help them. He told them to please tell his son and uncle that they were still alive and living in this refugee camp.

The next day, my uncle Noun came from his home in Chanthaburi (pronounced "Chan-buree"), Thailand, to see my father. My father explained to him that they could not go back to Thailand, because the Red Cross thought they were Cambodian. My uncle said, "Don't worry. Stay here, and we will come visit you all the time."

Meanwhile, my mom was trying to find out what had happened

to her kids. Noun told her that he had seen He Ty and Cole He in 1975, in Thailand.

Noun's father's brother from Chanthaburi went to find He Ty in Thailand. He asked the people where he had gone. He Ty's sister told him he'd gone to the United States with my brother in 1975. My uncle returned to tell my mom that her brother and son had gone to the United States.

She was given the address of where they lived in the States, and my mom wrote a letter, which He Ty eventually received in Ellensburg, Washington. He wrote back to my mom and then went to a Methodist church to find a sponsor for three people, which is what she thought was left of my family.

After mailing a letter a year earlier, my mom found out through the Red Cross that my sister was alive in France. When my mom received a letter from my sister, my mom wrote to her brother in the United States and told him they had found one more kid. Another was added to the list.

For two years, my mom and dad moved back and forth to different refugee camps. During this time, my mom continued asking people if they had seen or heard of her children. One day, some Cambodian Freedom Fighters came to visit the refugee camps. These soldiers, who had come to recruit kids for the Freedom Army, told my mom that not only did they know me but that I was the great leader of a Special Force and that I fought every day to get people out of the Killing Fields. My mom sent a letter back with them.

They brought that simple letter back to the Freedom Camp and changed my life.

30 Drop One, Take One

That special night in 1983, after reading my mom's letter, I thought, *Whoa, my mom found me!* Immediately, my thought then was, *I cannot live as if "Tomorrow I'm Dead" anymore.*

I wrote a letter to my mom and told her that I was still alive, that I'd had good rest and good food. I told her that I was helping people escape from the Khmer Rouge.

I told my crew that day that my mom had found me. I took the letter and went to see the Big Boss. "I want to go see my parents in the Thai refugee camp," I told him. "We've been split apart since April 1975."

The Big Boss said, "You stay here, Bun. I'll go get your parents and bring them here."

I said, "No, my mom doesn't want to hear bombs anymore. Let them stay there, where it's safe from this war."

I walked away and went to my room. As I lay there, I was scared. I thought about what I had been doing—fighting, getting trapped, stepping on mines. I thought, *I want to see my parents. I do not want to fight anymore. I do not want to die now.*

I thought about what the Big Boss had told me, but I tried to forget my parents after that—we were leaving in the morning to get more people out of Cambodia. I had to think of my soldiers.

One month later, after coming back from a second mission, there was another letter on my bed. My heart jumped—another letter from my mom! That day, I just sat and read the letter all day. She told me about my family, that they missed me, and that they had found my brother Cole He. That day, my heart filled up. I wanted to go find my mom. I wanted to get out of here. I went to the Big Boss again and told him I had gotten a second letter from my mom. I told him I wanted to go to my parents, and then I would come back.

My boss told me that I couldn't go. He would go instead. He told me that if I went away, my soldiers would be left with no one to watch over them.

I told the Big Boss to give me two weeks, and then I would come back, but he said, "No, your soldiers need you."

Once again, I tried to forget that letter. I talked to my soldiers and made jokes. Then we went on another mission into Cambodia.

Two days later, we got trapped by the Khmer Rouge. This one was very bad. They had us surrounded. I thought, *Oh-oh! My mom just found me, and now I am trapped. Is this my day to die?*

My soldiers came to me and asked, "What can we do? We are surrounded."

I knew help was two days away. We were very far into Cambodia. By the time help reached us, we would be dead. At that moment, I tried to forget my parents and think only about how to save my crew.

All thirty in my crew got together and prayed. We set up our equipment to get ready to go. All we needed was a four-hundred-foot gap in the line. I pulled everyone together with me and told them that we would use every single bullet and bomb to get through the circle in one narrow spot. We prayed together again and then dropped all our food and supplies on the ground so that we could move fast and bust through the circle. It was our only chance to survive.

With our AK-47s firing 120 rounds in seconds, we ran toward the Khmer Rouge, screaming and emptying our guns, clip after clip, until we had passed the line of soldiers. Bullets were flying everywhere. The Khmer Rouge couldn't lift their heads above the ground, or they would have been sprayed by our bullets. In training, I taught my soldiers how to tape sixty-round clips together on their AK-47s, so that as soon as they fired through one clip, they could pull it out, flip it over, shove it back in, and go through another sixty rounds. In their pockets were two more clips. This way, they could fire 240 rounds in a matter of seconds.

As we ran through the hole, screaming and shooting, Khmer Rouge lay dead on the ground. We ran into the jungle to get away from the return fire and kept running until we were scattered everywhere.

After we were out of range of the bullets, we started to look for each other to make sure everybody was okay.

I was looking for my crew when I heard big bombs coming in. I listened and realized these were Vietnamese bombs from tanks. The Vietnamese had heard the firefight and were zoning in on us. I said to my crew, "Oh, we are in big trouble now!"

We hid behind trees to protect us from the bombs. When it got quiet, we went looking for the rest of our crew. Three hours later, we still hadn't found them. We shot guns as signals. We had twenty-five people. Five were missing.

I told my crew to hang in there and not split up. We again shot in the air three times to signal. No response. We shot three more. Then we heard three shots from far away!

We shot back and then went to find the other five. We got to them and no one was hurt, so we went home.

When we returned, I went to the Big Boss and told him we had lost the fight this time. We had been trapped and had to blast through to get out. Then I asked him, "Can I go see my parents now? Please? Can I go?"

My boss said, "No, Bun, you have work to do. Your parents are safe and fed. You stay here with your soldiers. They need you."

That day, I told the Big Boss that if a third letter came, I would have to go. He still said that I could not go, that my life was as a soldier now. We lived together, slept together, and died together.

Two weeks later, the third letter arrived. My mom said that

I needed to come see them right away. She talked about how my brother had grown.

I went for a walk to a quiet place to think and read the letter again. I thought, *Do I go or stay with my soldiers?*

I had been to Cambodia too many times. I'd fought the Vietnamese and captured them alive. I'd fought the Khmer Rouge and captured them alive. I thought about a mission when some of my crew had gotten hurt, and the Big Boss had made me do five hundred push-ups. Another time, one of my soldiers was killed, and my boss made me run around a field until I could not pick up my legs. On every mission, I did all I could to keep my soldiers from getting hurt. I taught them everything, every minute, every hour of every day about how to stay alive.

I took care of them. And they stayed alive for three years of fighting Khmer Rouge and Vietnamese—twenty-four hours a day, seven days a week. I sat by a tree and talked to myself. I told myself my own story. How many times had I escaped death? All the fighting; all the narrow escapes. Every time my boss gave me more soldiers, I taught them how to treat the animals, the plants, and to be good to all people. I taught them how to fight, how to protect themselves, and how to protect all of us. Now, the fighting was getting worse. There were no more people to rescue, just soldiers fighting each other every day. It no longer made sense to risk our lives.

Now, my parents had found me. I wondered what would happen if I just walked away from this place. What would happen to all my best friends, my soldiers, my people? What would they do?

I answered myself, "I have old friends still here who can take care of these kids." I picked up my cap that read "Tomorrow I'm Dead." I closed my eyes and threw the cap down by the tree. I did not want to see that sign anymore. I grabbed the patch of the crossbones on my shoulder and ripped it off. I did not want to see it anymore. I could no longer say the words, "Tomorrow I'm dead."

That was it. I got up and walked back to my room. I talked to myself the whole way. "I have not lied to anyone. The third letter came, and now I have to go. I have to do it."

It was difficult for me to walk away from my soldiers. I sat down many times and took deep breaths. From 1977 until now, I'd been in this jungle. I knew everywhere to go. I knew where the mines and bombs were. I had put them in and taken them out. I had trained the soldiers how to do this.

I got up and walked the rest of the way to my room. That day, I wrote 300 letters, plus one for the Big Boss. I addressed the letters and piled them on my bed. I cleaned up my bed and put my gun and uniform next to my letters. I took the "Tomorrow I'm Dead" patch off my uniform. This time, I was not dead.

That night, I wrote everything down. I thought of how I had told the Big Boss that if a third letter came, I was gone. I prayed that he would understand what I had to do. I folded my uniform and set my AK-47 on my bed. I looked at my special rifle. I had never killed a human being with it. In all the times I fought with the Khmer Rouge, I shot over their heads and caught them alive. It was not good to kill a human. A good teacher had taught me that when I was twelve years old. I had never forgotten. Maybe that is how I survived five years of bullets, mines, bombs, jungle, and enemy soldiers.

Next to my AK-47, I set the two cans of gold I had collected over the last couple of years. I placed a note next to them, telling the Big Boss to take one of the cans to Thailand and to use the money to buy food and clothes for the people in the camp. I said to use half of the other can for my soldiers and the other half for him. I kept one gold necklace for myself.

That night when I woke up to leave, one kid, named Hood, asked me where I was going. I said to him, "Get your gun and come with me. Get one pair of clothes, and put them in your bag."

"Where are we going?" Hood asked.

"Just get your clothes and let's go."

"Where's your crew?" he wanted to know.

"We don't need a crew. This is just a small mission," I told him.

At ten o'clock, we walked away under a full moon. I knew that when my crew woke up, they would wonder where I was.

An hour later, we got to the second Cambodian front line. It was dark. They asked who we were and where we were going. I told them I was Bun.

"Oh, Bun!" they said. "Where is your crew?"

I repeated what I'd told Hood: "I don't need a crew, because it's just a small problem."

They let me through. Hood and I walked toward Thailand. After we were out of sight of the front line, I told Hood I was leaving the army.

"Does your crew know about this?" he asked.

"They know nothing."

"Bun, are you sure about this?"

"You can go back," I told him.

"No, I'll stay with you to keep you safe," Hood said.

"We have another border to cross—the Thailand border. This time, make sure not to say anything. Keep quiet and let me do all the talking. The Thai border will be dangerous."

I was not afraid of anything that night. I wanted to see my parents. I had survived since 1975. I felt that nothing would stop me now.

A half hour later, we reached the border. Soldiers with M-16s stopped us and asked who we were. I answered them in Thai. I told them I was from Thailand and had gone into Cambodia to try to make some money but had wound up walking out late. I made sure my Thai was perfect, because if the soldiers thought we were Cambodian, they would shoot us on the spot.

In my pocket was a grenade and a gun. If the soldiers stopped us, I planned to throw down the bomb, scare them, and get through the post. My Thai fooled them, though. The soldiers told me to be careful in Cambodia, because there were lots of mines and bombs. They let us through and went back to talking to each other.

Hood and I slept that night on the side of a tree in the jungle. The sun came up at five o'clock. We set our guns down, took off our uniforms, and changed into Thai clothes. We walked straight to a two-story house and knocked on the door.

The homeowner asked, "Who are you?"

"We're neighbors, and we need water," I said. He invited us in, and we talked for a while. Then I told him the truth. "I need to get to my uncle's place in Chanthaburi."

"Why are you here?"

"It's a long story, but right now, I need your help getting to my uncle."

He wanted to know the story.

"In 1975, my family was separated by the Khmer Rouge. My parents escaped to a Thai refugee camp. I survived the Killing Fields, became a Freedom Soldier, and now I need to see my parents. I need you to take me to them."

He said, "I have no money. I am poor."

"You can have my gold necklace."

That morning, he took the necklace to a restaurant next to his house. He traded the necklace for money and then came back and got us a taxi. He told the driver that he would need his services all day long.

The driver asked, "How many passengers will there be?"

The man replied, "Four. Me, my brother, Bun, and Hood."

The driver said, "I will need to wait for twelve people. Otherwise, it isn't worth it."

The man asked, "How much is it for twelve people?"

The driver replied, "I make seven baht [Thai money] per person for a long trip."

The man told him, "I have one hundred baht."

The driver's eyes opened wide! Now he was very happy to drive us all day.

The taxi driver asked where we were going, and when we said Chanthaburi, the driver said, "No problem. I know where that is."

We had breakfast together and then went back to the man's house. I asked him to tell his wife and brother to come out. I pointed to the tree and told him about my guns. I told him they could have the guns—an AK-47, a pistol, and one grenade. The brother was very excited. The man gave the money to his wife.

After that, we headed for my uncle's in Chanthaburi. We drove four hours straight to where the saltwater met fresh water. We got to a spot where I remembered walking as a kid. My uncle had always said to me, "First stop, first turn."

We got out at the first stop and walked around. I saw an old man with gray hair in a field. I said to this man, "Hey, uncle, do you know of a man named Noun?"

To this day I cannot believe that the first person I saw was my uncle. He said, "Yes, I know this name. I am Noun! *Are you Bun? You are big!*"

My grandmother came out of the house. She hugged me and cried, "I cannot believe you are still alive." She ran into the house and came out with a picture of me, taken on my first day of school. She had saved it all these years.

My uncle stopped working and raced off on his motorcycle to tell my parents that their son was in his house.

My mom did not believe him; she said that her son was still in Cambodia, fighting. My uncle came back and told me, "Bun, you stay here. Don't go anywhere." He told the taxi driver to stay as well.

The next morning, I got up around six o'clock. My mom and dad showed up and knocked on the door.

I cried, "Mom!"

My mom looked at me without a smile. In a very serious voice, she said, "You stay right there."

Then my parents walked away without saying another word. I turned to my grandma after they left and asked her what had happened. "Why did they leave? Are they mad at me? They didn't even ask how I was or anything."

The next morning, the UN Red Cross knocked on the door. They brought paperwork into the house and asked me questions. "What is your name?"

"Bun Yom."

"You have a father. What is his name?"

"Heng Yom."

"What is your mother's name?"

"Heng He."

"What are your sisters' names?"

I replied, "Bo Pha Yom. I have just one sister."

"What is your brother's name?"

"Cole He."

I answered all the questions. They tried to trick me with the question about my sister, asking as if I had two sisters instead of just one.

The UN officer then said, "Bun Yom, it is clear you are their son."

I asked my uncle to talk to my friend, Hood. They talked for a while, and Noun said he knew that Hood's uncle was still in Thailand. He left to find him.

When Hood's uncle came to get him, Hood said to me, "Bun, you saved my life. I will never forget you."

Then I went in the UN vehicle to the Thai camp to meet my mom. The taxi driver followed us down there. Once we were inside the refugee camp, the UN office gave me a release form, and my mom came to pick me up.

I pointed at the man I'd first met and the taxi driver and told my mom that these two people had helped me find her. I told her the whole story of how they had gotten me here safely.

My mom called them over and gave them each five bags of rice. Each bag weighed sixty pounds. Then she gave them five thousand baht apiece. The Thai man said, "Thank you, but I cannot carry all this back with me in my taxi."

My mom said not to worry. She called a Thai soldier over and told him to follow the taxi driver back to his home.

A Thai army truck showed up to haul the rice back to the man's house. My mom told them to bring three soldiers along to protect the rice and money from robbers. She told him to let her know when they got home. The soldiers followed the taxi all the way home. When they arrived, the two men wrote a thank-you letter to my mom.

That night, I stayed with my mom for the first time in eight years. I talked about my decision to leave my soldiers and how I had survived the Killing Fields. Friends came over and filled up the house. As I talked, many people asked if I had seen their kids. I told them that there were many kids, but they were hard to recognize, because they were skinny and their hair had fallen out. I told stories like that all night.

My mom brought plates of good food and tea for the people. We ate and drank. I could not sleep at all that night. I was happy to be with my parents, but I missed my crew. I missed the jungle with the trees. This camp had no trees. We were in a hot field with small apartment houses—thousands of little box houses.

Being "home" again filled me with a new energy. No more bombs. No more bullets. No more walking through the jungle. No war.

There were ten thousand refugees in the camp. My dad told me the story of how they had escaped the Khmer Rouge. Little Chhay played behind me. He was now eight years old.

Five days later, my soldiers found me. They had a letter and a message from the Big Boss.

My last day as a soldier for the Cambodian Freedom Fighters

31 *My Mom Buys My Freedom*

When I arrived at the Thai refugee camp in December 1983, my mom was busy selling large volumes of rice and beans to Thailand. This food was left by the United Nations to feed thousands of refugees. There was too much food for the people, so Mom asked the Thai people if she could sell them the extra rice and beans and give that money to the refugees for clothes. They agreed.

As soon as I arrived, I offered to help her—I remembered being very good at math in school. Five days after being reunited, I went to work for my mom.

That same day, Cambodian Freedom Soldiers showed up and found me. They brought me my uniform and gun, all in a case, as if they were brand new. The soldiers told me they had come to get me and my family and take us back to the Cambodian Freedom Camp. My mom met with them and told them that we had been separated since 1975.

"Bun has to come back," one soldier said, "because since he left, his soldiers have had no energy or enthusiasm. They don't want to fight anymore."

"I taught my soldiers how to fight, survive, stay alive, and find the enemy," I told the Freedom Soldiers. "Before I found out about my mom, I wore 'Tomorrow I'm Dead' on my uniform. Because of that, I was able to put my life on the line every single minute of every single day. My life was about helping my crew and rescuing people from the Killing Fields—twenty-five hours a day, eight days a week, thirteen months a year. Now that I have found my mom, I don't want to die. Now I am scared to fight. I have seen too many dangerous places and have been near too much trouble. Now, I have to walk away from that place of war and be with my family. It is very hard to do this.

"Please tell my crew and my soldiers that my mom found me, so I am staying with my parents right now. I will help them now, but I no longer will help with my muscles and technique. I help my mom with her business. Tell my boss and crew that I will send money to them. Sometime, I will go see them. I just don't know when."

One of the five soldiers told me that if I didn't go back with them, they didn't want to go back either, because their boss would kill them.

I told them, "That is not true. We are Cambodian Freedom Soldiers. We don't kill anybody, except Khmer Rouge, when we have to."

"After you left, the Big Boss wasn't happy," the soldier said. "He could not find anyone to replace you. He said that he considered you as his son. He is a tough 'bullets-look-like-rubber' type of man, and he believed in you. He felt that he and you shared some of the same gifts."

"I spent all those years fighting day and night in all kinds of weather," I said. "It was very hard. Now I need to take a break. I will go see the Big Boss sometime."

For four hours, the soldiers pleaded with me. I told the five Freedom Soldiers that I had to go outside for a little bit. I went to talk to my parents. Then my parents took over and talked with the soldiers, while I went out and played with the people in the refugee camp. An hour later, I checked and my parents were still talking to the soldiers. Two hours later when I looked, the soldiers were finally gone.

I went to my mom and asked, "How did you get them to go?"

"I gave each soldier five thousand baht in Thai money. I told them to take the money and go back home."

That is how my mom bought my freedom from the Cambodian Freedom Army.

Two weeks later, I received over three hundred letters from my soldiers and the people of my neighborhood. It took over one week to read the huge pile of letters. I wrote three hundred letters back. It took me a couple of days to write a short letter to each person. I also sent one hundred baht to each of them. After that, I carried in my bag the pile of letters my soldiers sent whenever I went somewhere. Most of the letters were complaints about my absence. The soldiers from my former unit said they had lost motivation. They missed hearing my voice, seeing me, and missed my leadership. I wondered if the Big Boss had put them up to writing these letters in order to persuade me to come back.

I stayed with my parents in the camp for three months. Soon, the UN Red Cross told me that three months was the maximum that a refugee could stay in a camp. We had to move to another camp. We headed to Kowedung, Thailand, to another refugee camp. When we arrived, they set up a small house for us. There was a large warehouse in camp for dividing food for all the refugees. The people in charge of the warehouse approached me and asked if I would help with dividing the beans, rice, fish, chicken, and vegetables for the refugees.

At the camp, many robberies had taken place during the night. The problem was so bad that people were unable to sleep. The camp's special police knew I had been a Freedom Soldier, and they asked me to help them catch the robbers. We would meet after the sun went down and then wait as a group to catch the robbers. In this way, we would help the people.

Doing this, I managed to stay busy, helping out at the camp. During the day I fed the people, and during the night I captured robbers so the camp could sleep. I did this for six months.

After all the years of catching Khmer Rouge alive, catching the robbers was easy. Some of them were Cambodian, some were Laotian, and some were Vietnamese. When we caught them, we took them aside and scared them. We explained that if they were caught again, we would cut off a finger. We then tied them next to a tree to scare them really bad. After half a day stuck there, we released them. There was no jail to keep them.

My mom stayed home and rested in this camp. Chhay played in the dirt, while my dad spent the day talking with friends. The camp was surrounded by barbed wire. There was nowhere to go and nothing to do. The toilet was a hole dug in the ground outside of our refugee house. We got our water from a water truck and carried it home in buckets.

Later that year, the UN Red Cross came to us and said we would be going to the Philippine camp. One day we boarded a bus. After a long, terrible ride, we got to an airport. I was scared, as I had never flown in an airplane. We took off at night, and I spent the whole flight with a paper bag on my knee, worried I would be sick.

Khon and I warming up for a one-hour running race

Me saying good-bye to my warehouse boss. May 1984.
The bus to Manila waits behind us.

32 The Philippine Camp

We arrived in Manila in the middle of the night and piled into a bus for the ride to a Philippine refugee camp. This drive was horrible. The road was winding, and people were tossed all over the bus. Many were throwing up. This went on all night. We tried to sleep, but it was impossible. The drive continued all the next day. We finally arrived at the refugee camp at three o'clock in the morning.

After everything was unloaded, refugee people approached my family and told them there was a room waiting for us. Everyone was still dizzy and sick from the bus ride. It took one week before we finally felt better.

We soon got to know many people at the camp—people from Cambodia, Laos, and Vietnam. One day, some friends invited us to go to the Cambodian temple. When we got there, I looked around and said, "This is not a Cambodian temple! It is a Vietnamese temple. The people speak Vietnamese, not Cambodian." Our new friends explained that during the war, the Vietnamese had taken away the Cambodian shrines and buried them in the dirt on a hill.

I went back to my place and told my parents that the Vietnamese had taken away the Buddha and buried it in the dirt. My father said, "That is not right." We decided to find the Buddha, dig it out, and put it in the temple again.

We visited with some Laotian people and told them our story.

That night, one hundred Laotian kids and one hundred Cambodian kids went down to the temple. We told the Vietnamese that we were there to take the temple back.

The Vietnamese told us that we could not come in.

"We will be back at ten in the morning to claim our temple," I said.

The next morning, the Vietnamese were there with more people, so we stormed the temple. We fought them with sticks, knives, and bare hands. We fought for two hours, bare-handed, fighting just like in the Bruce Lee martial arts movies. Finally, the Vietnamese ran away. The old people in our crew took the Vietnamese signs down and put up the Cambodian and Laotian shrines.

That day, we announced to the refugee camp that we had the temple back. A hundred people went to dig up the Buddha from the dirt, and then a thousand people carried Buddha to the temple on a wooden case that was built for transportation. That day, there was wonderful music and dancing. Old and young danced together all day and into the night. There was delicious food of all kinds, and everyone brought something special to eat—rice dishes, beef, vegetables, fruit.

For all the people, this was the happiest time in many years. In our culture, we had to have a temple to have a good life. Now we did. We made sure that the temple was protected. We stationed people to watch and protect it. To this day, if you are ever hungry, you can go to a Cambodian Temple in your city for free food. It doesn't matter which city or country. There will be a breakfast and a lunch there for you to enjoy.

The people at this camp knew that I could divide food, so they came to my home and asked me to help them divide food for the refugees. They told me that there were up to ten thousand refugees coming through the camp every day. These people needed to be fed.

At eight in the morning, I went to the warehouse and got food in a semitruck. Along with seven other workers, we divided up the food and gave it to the lines of people. After we divided food, we talked with friends. Then we went to the jungle and talked with Philippine friends. We took food for them that was left over from the morning meal. These very poor people had no money. They would give us wood in exchange—we used the wood to cook our food. They were happy to do this because I gave them so much food.

That month, I found my friend Khon. We were both in the temple. There were a thousand people inside, but I spotted him in the crowd. I shouted, "Hey, I know that guy. He was my crew number three leader!" I yelled, "Khon!"

He shouted back, "Bun!"

"How did you get here?" I asked him.

"I was captured by the Vietnamese in a fight. They took me to a village from which I escaped and came to the Red Cross. The Red Cross sent me to the refugee camp, which is how I got to Manila."

I told him the story of how I had left my soldiers in the night.

He said, "After you left, all the soldiers lost their will to fight. I was depressed as well."

I explained to him, "No one knew I went to the Big Boss many times to tell him that my mom had found me. I got scared and lost my will to fight, because I was now afraid to die. Fighting every day no longer made sense. I wanted to see my mom."

"After you left," Khon said, "the war got worse. There were many fights and many dead."

"Were any of my soldiers killed?" I asked.

"Yes, many."

I asked him the names; it was hard for me to believe that these kids were gone.

Khon said that the Vietnamese were now fighting us all the time—there were too many of them. Kill five soldiers, and ten more would come forward. Kill ten, and twenty would appear. This was the Vietnamese way. Their troops now occupied many Cambodian cities and villages.

The news of my soldiers' deaths was very hard for me to hear. I wanted to cry but could not cry that day. "What about Meng?" I asked. "I haven't seen Meng or my soldiers for a year. I miss them. I mailed a letter to them last week. Now they are gone."

Khon said to me, "Don't worry about Meng. He is alive and well. He married the lady he saved. They have a baby and are very happy."

Khon stayed with me after that. We talked at night about the war and our experiences. Khon told me his story about being captured by the Vietnamese. We talked about sleeping in the same camps, head to head. We talked about how we built a shelter together to sleep out of the rain and how during the night, the wind and a rainstorm had collapsed the roof. We had not slept that night—there had been no fire or any way for us to get warm. All of us were soaked. We laughed at that story.

We talked about the dam and planting rice. Khon told me not to think about it anymore. We had both been through too much.

After that, Khon helped me divide the food. No pay for either of us. We just volunteered.

Later, Khon said we should start running together in the morning. We started getting up at one in the morning and exercising for two hours before going off to run for an hour. We did this every morning before going to the warehouse at eight o'clock.

Sometimes we saw Vietnamese and Laotians running. On occasion, these runners would bump into us on the trail. One day we went to the Laotian house and asked why they did that.

I said, "Why did you hit me? I can run faster than you."

"So?" he said. "Are you sure?"

"Yes."

"You want to bet?" he asked.

"Okay."

He bet us one hundred pesos (Philippine money).

The next morning, we met the Laotians to race. We gave the money to our friends and had it waiting at the finish line for the winners. We ran for one hour straight. At the end of the race, we looked back at the Laotians and yelled, "Hey, you lost."

The next morning, we raced two Vietnamese. Then we raced some Mong (from Laos). The next day we raced a Cambodian team. We were making one hundred pesos every day. At night, we would go to Philippine restaurants and buy food, candy, coffee, and treats. Khon and I were together all the time, working, running, playing, and fighting in the temple. This was a very good time for us.

In the afternoon, I liked to play soccer (we called it football) on an international refugee team. I was the right wing of my team, jersey number seven. Two people on my team were very good. One was in the middle, and the other one was on left field. If the ball came to me, I would kick it to my friend in the middle, who was very fast.

Our opponents would try to break our legs, so I learned the technique of rolling on the ground to escape their kicks. The ground was bare—there was no grass. We made our own spikes by driving nails through our running shoes. We had to wear these because when it rained, the dirt turned to mud. There was only one rule in our soccer games—if the ball went off the field, the referee would bring it back and throw it to us. Otherwise, we could hit, and we could kick. There was no ambulance to haul away players with broken arms and legs. If we got hurt, we went home to our parents for help. The kicking was so hard that we broke at least two plastic balls each game. We paid old people in the camp to make us balls out of leather that wouldn't break.

Thousands of people watched us. They bet money on our games and cheered us, whether we won or lost.

Although the camp was not like my pre-1975 home, I was happy with it—new friends, good food, interesting things to do, no war—I could live again.

33   *How I Got to the USA*

After one of our runs, Manila was struck by a massive earthquake. People were running out of their houses into the road, asking, "What was that?" I had never experienced an earthquake, and it stuck in my mind as something very powerful. Things fell off shelves. My legs felt kind of rubbery, and I thought I was going to get sick.

Some of the people in the neighborhood told me that we lived on top of water, and below us was a huge fish that was shaking himself off. They laughed. After that, there was an earthquake every two or three days. Sometimes they were hard, and some were just a hum.

When anyone asked me what this shaking was, I told them the story about the big fish scratching his back. I said the fish was as big as a house.

To help pass the time in the camp, I volunteered to help out as a translator, as I spoke five Asian languages fluently and some French (but no English). I also devoted part of each day to teaching the kids in camp tae kwon do and karate. They loved this.

My uncle had contacted the United Nations and was trying to get our paperwork completed so we could leave the Philippines and go to the United States.

The boss at the warehouse liked me and let me run the food delivery. Each day, we brought in forty trucks of food for the people. We then divided up chicken, rice, vegetables, and beans for each person in each family. The boss said this was the first time the people did not suffer from too little food.

Luckily for me, I was very popular with many nice ladies in the camp. They liked me. Their parents liked me too and wanted me for a son-in-law. I said no, but I was still nice to the girls. Again, they cooked and cleaned for me. This allowed me to stay busy with racing, feeding the people, playing soccer, translating, teaching tae kwon do, and going with Khon to the city.

Day by day, we waited in the camp for permission from a sponsor to come to the United States. Finally, we received word that the Methodist church in Ellensburg, Washington, had found a sponsor who was ready to support our family in the United States.

Before we would be allowed to leave the refugee camp, my entire family had to take a special test, administered by the UN Red Cross.

We went to a room in a Manila hospital with a translator. We all waited in a long line. Then we walked past a curtain, one at a time. They had us take off all our clothes. We then stood naked in front of a Red Cross official, who sat there with a clipboard. Behind the curtain were translators: Cambodian, Laotian, and Vietnamese. The translators would tell us what to do, and the Red Cross official would watch us and write things down. I was told to lift my arms and turn around. The official looked at my whole body, every single part. He gave me a green card, which meant I was okay. Then I was allowed to put my clothes back on and go out.

My brother Chhay went in next and did this test. He didn't pass because he had chicken pox. He came out from the curtain with a red card. The people in line said, "Oh, they stopped you. You cannot be released to the USA."

We took my brother to a doctor. He told my brother that he had to go to a "monkey" jail far away from the people. They took him from my family and put him in a cell two miles from the camp. We went to visit and feed our little monkey every morning.

That week, we received word from the Red Cross that our sponsors thought we were scheduled to arrive and had waited at the airport for us. They did not know about my brother's illness. We contacted them and apologized for this. We told them that my brother had not passed the test because of chicken pox and that with good luck, we would arrive the following week.

I went back to work at the warehouse the next morning and told my boss that I would be leaving for the USA the next week. He was very sad. He said he had never seen anyone divide food so well for the people. He loved me and wanted me to stay and help the people. I told him I needed to go be with my family in the United States. He wrote me a wonderful letter of recommendation.

After a week in the monkey jail, my brother got the green light. I then went around saying good-bye to all my friends. Girls that had helped me with my clothes and food came to me and cried. My food leader cried when we said good-bye.

I told them, "This is my day to start a new life."

That day, I packed everything I would need to bring to my new life. Around my neck hung the IOM (International Organization for Migration) refugee identification card. I was wearing the one pair of clothes I would take to America. My backpack was full of paperwork and legal documents. I had no money—not one penny. We had given all our meager possessions away to the Philippine jungle people.

As we drove away from the camp, I looked out the bus window. I could not believe my eyes. We were winding along a steep, dangerous, narrow road, with huge cliffs below us. I looked down and was very scared. If the bus went off the road, we were dead. I had survived the Killing Fields and fought the Khmer Rouge and Vietnamese. I spent eight years in constant labor, and I'd dodged bullets and bombs—and I realized I might die right here in a bus crash. Once again, the people on the bus started throwing up on each other. Everybody was sick from the winding, scary road.

Finally, we got to the airport. Over eight hundred refugees were told to line up in different lines: Cambodian, Laotian, Mong, and Vietnamese. Then we boarded the plane. It was crowded. We were small and were put two to a seat. I got a seat in the middle by the window. As the airplane took off from the Philippines, I could look down on all the colors—the green and yellow of the trees, the blue of the water. I saw the houses getting smaller. That was it. Good-bye, Philippines. I was heading to new friends.

We arrived in Tokyo, and the refugees all headed in different directions. Some were going to France, Australia, or South Africa. Five hundred from my camp immediately boarded a giant plane headed for San Francisco, with no break. When I looked out the window, it was all blue. I kept looking at my watch. Twelve hours later, we still hadn't landed. On the big-screen TV, they played a cowboy movie over and over. I looked at my watch every hour for six more hours. We finally arrived in San Francisco. It was very cold. We were given jackets and a room to rest in. Five families, including mine, got on the next plane for the flight to Seattle-Tacoma (Sea-Tac) Airport in Seattle, Washington. At Sea-Tac, we got on a small plane. There was just my family and twelve tall white people. The flight from Seattle went straight up over the west side of the mountains of Washington State and then straight down the east side to Yakima. I looked out the window. There was a lot of green and a lot of square things. I had no idea what they were. Twenty hours after leaving our friends in Manila, we arrived in Yakima, Washington.

I saw my uncle with a vehicle at the airport. It was the first time I'd seen him since 1975. My brother Cole He was there too. He was huge with big muscles. He was a senior in high school. The last time I had seen him, he was ten years old.

The sponsors put us in cars and drove us to Ellensburg. There was already a house for us.

Me standing in the Philippine Cambodian temple with the rescued Buddha

I, a black belt, volunteer to teach tae kwon do and karate to kids in the Philippine camp. I did this in my spare time.

34 *Welcome to America*

On the first day in Ellensburg, many people came by to see us. I was confused—the sound of the airplane still was ringing in my ears. I couldn't do anything; I couldn't eat or sleep. I was very tight and nervous. The next morning, the sponsor took us to the doctor to make sure we were all okay. The doctor x-rayed me from toe to head. He found metal in my body; there was a piece of shrapnel in my leg. He told me that they would wait for a few years to take out the metal. (Five years later, when I went to have it removed, the x-ray showed no metal. The doctor and I had no idea where it went.)

Our house was on Ruby Street. My brother Cole He had been there since 1975. He took me and my parents around in his car, showing us the town. I told him my story as we drove around. At night, after we came back home, I went in to use the bathroom. I looked around at the room and the toilet. I looked in the toilet bowl; there was water in there. In the airplane toilet, there was just a bowl and a hole but no water.

I had been taught not to pee or poop on water. This was considered a bad thing to do to the water, so I went outside to the back porch and decided to "water" the plants.

I then went up to my room, turned on all the lights, and went to sleep. I had never slept in a room with lights before. My brother came up to our room and shut off the lights. I woke up; I had pulled my blanket over my head. I looked around me, and it was dark, so I got up and turned the lights back on. My brother woke up and turned the lights back off. I got up and turned them on again. Finally, he said, "What are you doing?"

I said, "I can't sleep with the lights off." I lay down to sleep but decided I needed to use the bathroom again. This time, I needed to poop, so I went in to use the toilet. I looked at the bowl again. I couldn't figure out how I could poop but not hit the water. I didn't know what to do. I wondered if I could poop outside. I did not know the rules in the United States, because no one had told me. In the Philippines and Cambodia, you could just go outside to the jungle. The bathrooms were just a hole in the ground.

I decided to use the toilet paper to fill the bowl. Then I climbed up on the toilet seat, with my feet on the lid. When I was done, I walked back in the bedroom.

My brother was awake and asked me why he hadn't heard any water running. He took me in the bathroom and gave me a lesson on how to use the toilet, American-style. After that, we crawled into bed. He let me leave the lights on.

I slept with the blankets over my head.

Our sponsors helped my family with trips to the store. We pushed two carts around the grocery store. The sponsor told us to buy anything we wanted, so we filled the carts with packages. We had no idea what we were buying. We just picked things that looked nice. The sponsor also gave us a phone and said to just push a button on the phone if we needed help.

Two months later, I felt better. I was no longer dizzy, but my legs were still sore from sitting in the airplane for twenty hours. Every night when I slept, I heard bombs all night. I could see my soldiers in my dreams. We talked, walked, played, and fought. I thought about the Khmer Rouge and almost dying so many times.

One night, I was screaming in my sleep. My brother woke me up and asked what happened. I told him I was having a nightmare. I was fighting in the jungle. I was screaming, "Go up! Catch them alive!"

I was sweating all over my body. After that, I couldn't sleep, so I went outside and sat by a tree for a long time. My brother came out about one in the morning and asked, "Why are you out here?"

"I cannot sleep," I answered. "I think about my crew."

"Bun, you are in America now. You do not have to think about that anymore."

"I heard bombs," I said.

He did not know what to say to me about that. Cole He had escaped the war.

I told my mom the next day that I could not sleep, and I was thinking about my soldiers. My parents told me that it was hard to walk away from a job like that. They said my soldiers were thinking about me too and that was why I was dreaming about them. I told them that maybe Meng was in charge of the soldiers now; I hoped my soldiers were okay.

One day a Cambodian friend, Bun Retha Ka, asked me, "Do you want to go to work?"

For three months, I had been receiving a welfare check for doing nothing. I laughed at him. I told him that I had just worked for five years straight, twenty-three hours a day, for nothing. I told him I was tired of working.

He laughed at me and explained that in America, you got paid to work. I told my mom, "Mom, a friend called and told me I would get paid to go to work."

She told me that this was true.

My friend Bun Ma came by, and when I told him about the job, he looked at me and said, "You are skinny and still sick, and you want to go to work in America? You are too small and too weak!" (I only weighed ninety-nine pounds at the time.)

The next day, my Cambodian friend picked me up to go work on a farm in Kittitas. After work, my friend brought me home and said he would pick me up the next morning at seven o'clock. The next morning, however, he found out that he had to go to a different job, but he wasn't able to tell me.

I went out in the morning to wait for my ride. He didn't show up. When I told my mom, she said I had better hurry up and run to the farm. I was supposed to be there by eight o'clock, so I took off running for the farm. It was ten miles away. A little over thirty minutes later, I raced up to the farm. A track coach later told me this was not possible. He said it would have broken all records! I told him I had the tattoo on my knees from my teacher and had sprinted the whole way, just like I had with Khon back in the one-hour Philippine races.

That day, we worked in eighty-degree heat, pulling weeds and digging dirt for the potato fields. That night, I ran the ten miles back home. When I got there, Mom had prepared a meal, and we watched TV. I wrote on the board that night that my pay was four dollars an hour. I had worked for eight hours, which meant I made thirty-two dollars! I said, "Whoa, that is more than I made in five years in Cambodia!"

The next day, my uncle got hold of me and asked me if I wanted to go to work at another job. I agreed. I didn't bother to tell him I was already working at the farm in Kittitas, so that day, I got another job that started at six in the evening. We were to clean up a meat factory after the workers went home.

The next morning, I ran off to the Kittitas farm and did my job in the heat. When I got off work, I ran back to meet my uncle at the meat factory. I got there ahead of my uncle. When he showed up, we cleaned for two hours.

The next day, a Cambodian cousin, who worked at Twin City Foods, asked if I wanted another job. I said yes. This job started at 8:00 p.m. and ended at 6:00 a.m. After I finished at that job, I ran out to the farm and worked until 5:00 p.m. Then I ran back to downtown Ellensburg and went to work at the meat factory with my uncle for two hours. Then I ran home and ate some dinner that my mom had prepared. By 8:00 p.m., I was at Twin City Foods, where I picked up corn on an assembly line until 6:00 a.m. Then I raced back home and slept for an hour, woke up, and ran to the farm in Kittitas.

My dad heard I was doing this and said, "Bun, you are going to drop dead."

I told him, "Dad, in my army I worked twenty-four hours a day, with my life on the line every day, and never got paid. I helped people in the camps and never got paid. Here, I am making money for the first time."

Sometimes when I worked on the assembly line, I would think about my time with my soldiers. Sometimes I thought about funny things, like the long plane flight to America. Twenty hours, with eight hundred people using the bathroom on that plane. I wondered where all that stuff went.

That year I worked many jobs and made a lot of money. I took the fourth welfare check back to the office with a Cambodian translator because I was making so much money. I returned the check and told them I was working three jobs and making much more than welfare.

The lady in the office said, "Why are you doing that? You are supposed to be taking it easy and recovering."

The work on the Kittitas farm ended that winter, so I replaced that job by cleaning a restaurant from 9:00 a.m. until noon. Then I would go to work at Washington Beef Factory from 1:00 p.m. to 5:00 p.m. and then run home and eat dinner before racing off to work at Twin City Foods from 6:00 p.m. until 6:00 a.m.

I would go home in the morning and get about an hour's sleep before going to clean up the restaurant.

During my spare time, I did wood work and yard work and helped out at the Methodist church. I worked like this seven days a week. If I stayed busy like this, I did not think as often about the Killing Fields, the bombs, or my soldiers.

Every Friday, I gave my mom my money. I would ask her for five dollars to buy candy. The candy was good for running and during break times at all my jobs.

This was how I spent my first two years in America. No English, TV, or girlfriend. Just running, working, and making money to give to my family and friends.

The year 1984 was a good one for my family. Except for my brother Phon, who had not been found, all my mom's kids had survived the terrible crimes of the Khmer Rouge. My sister was doing well in France. Cole was a senior in high school, Chhay was learning English in school, and I was working many jobs and having fun. My dad enjoyed talking with his friends and family.

Every single day, I was thankful that my mom had found me. Without her letters, I do not know how much longer I would have survived the war. For eight years, my mom never gave up hope that she would find her children. The fact that she found me is proof that in life, no matter how tough it gets, you have to hang in there. Never, ever give up.

Cambodian Identification

The Yom family (minus oldest brother, Phon) reunited in Tacoma,
Washington, in 1997. My mom (second from left) found my brother Cole He
in the United States in 1980 and my sister, Bo Pha, in France in 1981.

35 *A Last Blessing*

Phon Yom, the oldest of my siblings, was found in Cambodia in 1996, through my mom's continuous efforts to contact agencies, friends, and relatives in the hope of finding her son. Phon Yom's story is also an amazing tale of survival. Phon labored in the Killing Fields until 1979, when he managed to escape to the Vietnamese side during a battle between the Khmer Rouge and Vietnamese soldiers. After recuperating, Phon joined up with the Vietnamese army so that he could have food. He fought with the Vietnamese army against the Khmer Rouge until 1981.

In a twisted turn of fate, his last day as a soldier was the day my Freedom Soldiers encountered Phon's Vietnamese patrol. My Special Force had Phon's troops surrounded and quickly set up their cannons to destroy the Vietnamese positions. Minutes before the bombs landed, Phon sensed trouble and escaped from the entrapment.

Having no idea my brother was there, I proceeded to pinpoint bomb the exact spot where Phon had been standing just moments before. This brush with certain death convinced Phon to leave the Vietnamese army and find a better life. He wound up living with a friend in Cambodia and started a bicycle repair shop. I called Phon in 1996 and talked about life and our last days in the army. During that call, I figured out it was I who had bombed my brother into some sensibility. A fitting ending, indeed.

My brother Phon Yom

36 Conclusion

I do not understand why all the members of my family were spared while so many others perished. I do know that my family and my teachers taught my brothers, sister, and me to do good for all people, to walk a straight road, and to help people and never cheat them. These things I remembered, even in the darkest hours of the Killing Fields and the war. Maybe it was these things that kept me alive and kept my family alive. The experiences of the Killing Fields will always be with me, but I always try to look ahead. Here in America, I have a new start and new friends. Coming from Yakima to Ellensburg through the Yakima River Canyon reminded me somewhat of Cambodia—the canyon walls, the running water. Maybe I had brought a little of my homeland with me.

About the Author

Bun Yom has been a fixture in the Ellensburg, Washington, community since 1984. He is married and has three children, a son and two daughters. After working for a time as groundskeeper at the Kittitas County Fairgrounds, Bun and his family started a Thai food restaurant, which he later sold and invested the money in an automobile repair garage. When this business failed during the great recession following 2008, he has since spent his time and energy working on his books.

Bun demonstrates for a friend how to fly.

COMING SOON

Welcome to America

by Bun Yom

Bun Yom's sequel to *Tomorrow I'm Dead*, titled *Welcome to America*, will be available soon. After surviving the Killing Fields and the endless wars in Cambodia, Bun finds himself in Ellensburg, a small rodeo town in central Washington, facing a new adventure and a whole new set of challenges in a world that most of us take for granted. Accustomed to a twenty-five-hour-a-day, eight-days-a-week pace, Bun spends three years working around the clock. He becomes a well-respected curiosity piece in the community: "the little Cambodian refugee who runs to all of his jobs." In 1986, Bun starts a full-time job as a groundskeeper for the Kittitas County Fairgrounds in Ellensburg, where he devotes his unstoppable energy to his work and to helping all people. Bun is soon promoted to head groundskeeper and faces challenges that even Bun's humor, wit, and endurance are not prepared for. Bun's amazing saga continues, as our saintlike, five-foot-three, working-class hero tries to "hang in there" and help out in a world that is sometimes very hard to understand.

Printed in the United States
By Bookmasters